LEADING EDGE

STRATEGIES FOR DEVELOPING AND SUSTAINING
HIGH-PERFORMING TEAMS

ALISON GRIEVE AND JENNI MILLER

First published in Great Britain by Practical Inspiration Publishing, 2023

© Alison Grieve and Jenni Miller, 2023

The moral rights of the author have been asserted

ISBN   9781788604604   (print)
        9781788604611   (epub)
        9781788604598   (mobi)

All rights reserved. This book, or any portion thereof, may not be reproduced without the express written permission of the author.

The diamond charter, the dynamic diamond and the accelerators were designed by Alison Grieve and Jenni Miller and illustrated by Andrew Pagram (Beehive Illustration).

Every effort has been made to trace copyright holders and to obtain their permission for the use of copyright material. The publisher apologizes for any errors or omissions and would be grateful if notified of any corrections that should be incorporated in future reprints or editions of this book.

Want to bulk-buy copies of this book for your team and colleagues? We can customize the content and co-brand *Leading Edge* to suit your business's needs.

Please email info@practicalinspiration.com for more details.

Contents

About the authors v
Foreword vii
Introduction: Why high-performing teams? xi

PART ONE: High-performing team dynamics 1
Chapter 1: The principles and dynamics of high-performing teams 3
Chapter 2: Reason 27
Chapter 3: Results 43
Chapter 4: Routines 61
Chapter 5: Relationships 83
Chapter 6: Resilience 119

PART TWO: Leadership and team development 145
Chapter 7: Leading a high-performing team 147
Chapter 8: Accelerators and interferences 163
Chapter 9: Team composition for high performance 179

Conclusion 203
Acknowledgements 209
Bibliography 211
Index 215

About the authors

Alison Grieve and Jenni Miller work with leaders in large multinational companies to help transform company culture and create differentiated performance.

Alison is a sought-after learning professional, working globally across multiple industries at all levels. She drives performance for clients by raising the capabilities of their people and teams to world class in a unique way every time. Her depth of knowledge and skill in the talent and people space is unparalleled, where she creates change that really works. Highly qualified, she is a Korn Ferry master associate, a NLP Master Practitioner and a certified Executive Coach (ICF PCC). She is a founding director at Management Dynamics and a team coach, working with leaders and teams in some of the most successful businesses on the planet.

Jenni has extensive experience in the talent and leadership development arena, working with multinational organizations around the world. She is fascinated by the people and organizations that make a great, lasting impact on the world and she is renowned for her unshakeable pragmatism and ability to create performance through people and teams. She has a post-graduate diploma in learning and development, is a certified NLP trainer and a certified coach (ICF ACC). She is also founding director at Management Dynamics and a team coach.

Together, Alison and Jenni have developed a blueprint for success that captures how the greatest leaders and teams think, act and communicate to overcome mediocrity and drive outstanding personal and organizational performance.

Their findings are based on original research with hundreds of teams, and they frequently write and run webinars on leadership and teams based on their research and experiences. They regularly appear as guests on podcasts and webinars and won four awards in 2022, including the STEVIE's Women in Business Award for Company of the Year.

Foreword

Frederic Debrosses, General Manager Middle East, Africa, Global Business Development, JDE Peet's

One could say that meeting Alison 10 years ago in South Africa was a coincidence. I would reply that everything happens for a (good) reason! During this time, I was navigating the challenges of leadership, diversity and team performance in a pretty complex, yet amazingly inspiring context. Alison supported me with the facilitation of a great and memorable workshop not only for my leadership team, but also for me as a leader in a global and diverse organization. As for Jenni, I met her virtually a decade later, in the midst of the pandemic, feeling once again this common drive, energy and passion about optimizing team performance and unleashing the unlimited potential of people. Besides being passionate, Alison and Jenni have gained a vast, multifaceted and multicultural experience through their multiple interactions with hundreds of teams and leaders. As a result, they are uniquely placed and privileged to share their hard-won expertise, insights and learnings with teams around the world.

I have been building, engaging and leading diverse teams for more than 20 years across geographies, broadening and deepening my understanding for team dynamics. Every place and every context is different, yet there is one thing that is true everywhere: a team is much more than the sum of its parts. Forming, empowering and leading a high-performing team taps into the ability of leaders to weave distinct individualities together and unleash the power of collaboration where everyone becomes the best version of themselves. Teamwork, when well-orchestrated, is a key factor of success, but in its disharmony is one of the most common reasons for organizations failing to thrive, harness and take advantage of market opportunities. For those of you who are ready to try, I can guarantee that a high performing team will bring you a unique competitive advantage, that will adapt, sustain and endure in all different circumstances.

With *Leading Edge*, Alison and Jenni offer simple strategies and tools as well as case studies to illustrate and ultimately drive outstanding individual and collective performance to new heights. As a leader you always have a very unique and special role to play in that you may hold your team back or enable it towards a greater performance, all dependent upon your attitude, guidance and choices. While the state of sustained high team performance remains virtually magical and often difficult to explain, you may find that this book is designed and written with the goal of making it more relatable, practicable and ideally replicable. It is all about how you decide to think, act and communicate to inspire and foster a well-calibrated, inclusive and optimally performing team.

My personal message is that self-awareness and authenticity are two critical foundations that will only enable you to appreciate, embrace and extend what you will gain out of this seminal book.

Read, unlearn, relearn, apply... and enjoy, cherish and celebrate your team's high performance.

Neil Molyneux, Technical innovation Director, Pepsico

Have no doubt, your high-performing team development journey is one that stretches way beyond what can be currently envisaged... in all honesty, you should only step into leadership challenges of this kind if you have the energy that comes from a burning passion to make a difference, when you have a fuel and zest for life, when those around you realize it can be better, believe it will be better and then move forward to improve delivery. *Leading Edge* not only offers a compass to navigate this, but it's also a hugely helpful reference to set direction and course correct, it shines a light on the pathway by providing a very clear, succinct and structured framework to help surface tension, identify cultural and performance drivers and really get under the skin of what's going on and what's important to the team so you can act.

If you're ready, want to take action and start modelling those behaviours to give yourself the edge... this is a must read to create that momentum!

Erik Schmidt, former CHRO, Pandora

It's rare in a career you find an organization so in need of a major overhaul to be able to deliver its purpose for its consumers. And yet this was where we found Pandora (the world's largest jewellery brand by volume) back in 2019. This overhaul was needed to safeguard the loyalty of millions of consumers in nearly 100 countries and the livelihoods of over 25,000 employees and their families around the world. The global reset, which started in 2020, meant a new operating model, over 60% new leadership talent, new cultural values, reset performance expectations around leadership KPIs, new reward infrastructure and much more – in short, a whole new ecosystem.

And yet as any football (soccer) commentator will tell you, just having the best talent in the world by itself will not guarantee you success! Many coaching careers have ended abruptly on that myth. Having amassed the talent drawn from world-class businesses globally, many leaders in their fields, ensuring new and existing talent blended well at Pandora was key. New leaders and sometimes whole new teams needed to get from form, through a set of global lockdowns preventing the more human social interactions that help build lasting bonds, to perform in a quick and effective way – consumer sentiment and employee livelihoods depended on it and shareholders were looking for the financials to return to greatness.

It was on this journey that we first crossed paths with Alison and Jenni – two talented professionals, early in the lifespan of their entrepreneurial creation and with a compelling model based on data and strong facilitation. We were taken by their values, which fit with ours, their commitment to measuring impact and their track record of success in other organizations. They were invited to go large across the top three career bands globally in Pandora – at one point they were helping 27 different leadership teams everywhere from Panama to Thailand to Sydney. This resulted over time in a nearly 10% increase in employee-reported team strength. In 2022 it also contributed to Pandora delivering four record quarters of trading performance and top decile employee net promoter score results!

Introduction: Why high-performing teams?

In over 25 years of working with teams, we've noticed that the rate of change and the complexity that teams are operating in has increased dramatically. Teams have always been important to organizations but the requirement for enhanced collaboration and collective problem-solving has never been greater. The challenges we all face have become – and will continue to be – so complex that, without excellent teamwork, organizations will fail to thrive and make the most of potential opportunities. Whether this is coming up with new routes to market, innovative products, overcoming supply chain issues, retaining people or sustaining growth during challenging times, teams are at the heart of the solution.

What is it that teams bring to organizations? At their simplest, teams are an organizational structure to manage work in the most efficient and cost-effective way. At their best, they're a vehicle for innovation, complex problem-solving and superior decision-making. High-performing teams are a true competitive edge for any organization. A thriving team will create superior solutions – faster, better, stronger – than others. Which means your team will beat their competition every time. High-performing teams are self-sustaining. They manage what to other teams would be a dip in productivity, so that performance is never impacted.

Everyone gets the importance of having high-performing people (as individuals) in their team. We've all heard of the 'war for talent', and this results in leaders fighting to get the best people into their teams. However, if leaders only focus on the individuals in their teams, they're missing out on tapping into the competitive edge that a high-performing team of people delivers together. A high-performing team isn't just the sum of its high-performing parts. It taps into something more and unleashes the power of collaboration and the spark that people working together effectively create. Every team we've worked with talks about the idea of *potential* in the team. Even when they're a good, solid team already, they sense that there's more that the team is capable of – it just needs to be unlocked and the team would be unstoppable. A sign of a high-performing team is that they still feel this way, even when they're smashing their targets and achieving more than they or the organization ever felt possible. A high-performing team always wants more and they know that more is possible by working smarter, not harder.

What is high performance?

When we talk about high performance, teams often ask us what we mean – how do we define it? Many teams assume, at first, that performance is all about the numbers, the key performance indicators (KPIs) or the objectives that the team needs to achieve. And that seems quite intuitive, doesn't it? Surely the organization measures a team's success in this way? Our challenge to those teams is to ask the question: 'And if your team is meeting your objectives, but it feels awful to be a part of this team, is that okay? Is that still high-performing?' And the answer is always 'no'. In our view, high performance – getting your team to the edge of their potential and beyond – must include not just achieving some objectives but also great dynamics in the team – *why* they exist, clarity on *what* they need to deliver, and *how* they work together to get things done. When these two aspects – achievement of objectives and great dynamics – are present in a team, they can not only achieve or exceed their objectives, but they can also sustain that level of achievement over a long period and through challenging times.

Most teams find it hard to articulate what high performance would look like for them. They also may worry that higher performance means more work. This is just not the case. In fact, higher performance should mean working smarter, not harder. Many teams aren't far removed from this and could therefore be described as a good team. It won't take much to get them to high performance, but this doesn't happen by chance. When a team unlocks their potential, their motivation becomes self-sustaining.

The VUCA[1] world

Let's consider the context in which teams operate today. The term VUCA has been used for decades to describe Volatility, Uncertainty, Complexity and Ambiguity. Originally coined to describe the challenges the Cold War posed the US Army and the new ways in which it needed to approach the conflict, this term has increasingly been used in organizations. This is because the context in which organizations operate can increasingly be described as VUCA for two key reasons: globalization and digitalization. Globalization means that more and more organizations operate from a global perspective and are dependent on people connecting

---

[1] www.vuca-world.org/where-does-the-term-vuca-come-from/

across the world to get things done. Digitalization means that the omnipresence of information and the digital connectedness of the world create complexity and pressure to respond ever more quickly. Teams are now more multinational than ever before, operating in a global context. They're likely to rely on and interact with others in different parts of the world. They're also enabled by digitalization to communicate and make decisions. Many decisions require deep analysis of vast amounts of information. This creates more complexity than ever before for teams.

A team of high-performing individuals, while on the face of it attractive, is no longer enough to meet these challenges. A high-performing team is required to thrive in the VUCA world. However, organizations aren't generally set up to support a high-performing team. They're set to support high-performing individuals instead. From recruitment, to onboarding, to performance management, to reward, to development, to exit, everything is geared up to a one-on-one relationship between the leader and the individual team member. In this book, we challenge you as a leader to think differently about your role in your team and what you will need to do to get them to and sustain high performance. You will probably need to do this in the context of an organization that still thinks primarily about leading and managing individuals. However, what we've found is that your individual high performers crave being part of a high-performing team. So, by investing time and effort in your team and in yourself as a leader, you're also investing in them as individuals.

> 'Having or being part of a high-performing team has to be embraced, welcomed and understood to be a fundamental ingredient in your success.'
>
> **David Allen**
> **Managing Director, Pacific and Greater Asia, Pandora**

The need for high-performing teams

High-performing teams deliver at least three things to an organization: greater innovation, complex problem-solving and superior decision-making.

Greater innovation

Innovation is rarely achieved successfully by one person alone and it requires a team to make an idea reality. Teams take an idea, make it even better and create a plan together to turn it into something tangible, with organizational benefits. It's about experimenting, taking risks, learning from mistakes and failures and embracing a mindset of possibility. Alone, one person can demonstrate some of these traits but is unlikely to be able to sustain this over time or realize the value to the organization. One person might have a great idea but taking that idea from concept to reality requires teamwork; they can rarely (if ever) do it alone. A high-performing team creates a playground for ideas – a space in which experimentation is embraced and risks are taken.

Complex problem-solving

One person can easily solve a simple problem by themselves. Complex problems, however, require different methods of approaching them. High-performing teams thrive on solving complex problems and utilize the strengths of the team to achieve a better solution. They use the diversity of perspectives in the team as well as the mental capacity of the whole team to approach the problem from a different angle.

Superior decision-making

High-quality, timely decision-making is essential in organizations – if decisions are made too late or if they're not made well, organizations fail. Often, we see teams that struggle to make decisions, have repeated conversations and don't move forward. Or we see leaders who are bottlenecks for decisions because their team defers all decision-making to them. We also see teams that make decisions at the wrong level in the organization – leaders are focused on the tactical at the expense of the strategic and disempower the people they lead. High-performing teams consistently make great decisions and they do this through trust, collaboration and constructive challenge. They also make the right decisions quickly and efficiently. They ensure that decisions are high quality by considering diverse opinions. This is a fundamental building block of the competitive edge a high-performing team can deliver.

Organizational benefits

The possible organizational benefits of high-performing teams are well researched and documented. Organizations see a drop in employee turnover when teams are cohesive and engaged.[2] Teams create a sense of belonging, collabo-

---

[2] K. Blanchard, *Leading at a higher level: how to be a high-performing leader* (2010).

ration and achievement, so high-performing teams are an organizational lever to reducing turnover.

Resources are usually limited in organizations, and when talking about this we include money, time, people and materials. High-performing teams make better use of the resources that they have and are more productive than other teams.[3] This is because high-performing teams think more creatively about how to use what they already have more effectively.

When people are part of a high-performing team, they're much more likely to be engaged, which means that they're more motivated and productive, which in turn delivers better organizational results.[4]

When people are more engaged, they're happier at work, which reduces absence and sickness.

As we've already established, complexity is an increasing part of our working lives and how to solve complex problems is a common organizational challenge. According to Ernst & Young, 'Almost 9 out of 10 companies… agree that the problems confronting them are now so complex that teams are essential to provide effective solutions.'[5] High-performing teams tackle complex challenges head-on.

Individual benefits

By extension, the organizational benefits lead to positive impacts on individual team members. High performance is something that's enjoyed by everyone – after all, who doesn't

---

[3] L. Wizeman, *Multipliers: how the best leaders make everyone smart* (2017).
[4] M. Buckingham and A. Goodall, *Nine lies about work* (2019).
[5] 'The power of many: how companies use teams to drive superior corporate performance', Ernst & Young, May 2013.

want to be a part of a high-performing team? When someone has a team around them, supporting them, they can achieve so much more than on their own. They're able to get to their own performance edge and beyond more easily. A leader of a high-performing team doesn't need to have all the answers and nor does an individual team member, as they can find the answer together. This means that they can take more risks, be more confident and achieve more together. This is where a team is greater than the sum of its parts.

The benefits to you

It's all very well having all these benefits for the organization and your team members, but what about you? Why bother investing your valuable time in developing your team to high performance? What's in it for you? First of all, let's explore what happens if you don't invest. If you don't create a high-performing team, the full accountability for the performance of your team lies with you. The team will look to you for the answers to everything. You'll find that you are repeating yourself regularly and fire-fighting problems. You'll get copied on every email, you won't be able to have a holiday without being contacted. Your diary will be full of meetings, most of which you'll leave feeling that they weren't the best use of your time. Imagine what a high-performing team could do for you – they'll be empowered to make the right decisions without you being involved. They'll know when to include you and will keep you sufficiently informed of issues without needing your direct input all the time. They can maintain this while you're taking time to rest and recharge. You'll have time to think and to focus on the strategic issues that add massive value to the organization and people's perception of your leadership capability. When you lead a high-performing team, it's easy to attract talent to the team – people will know about the reputation of your team and want to be part of it. You'll also keep people in the team for longer, as the benefits of being part of a high-performing team create a deep sense of loyalty to and ownership of the team. In short, you'd be crazy not to!

The conditions for success in a high-performing team

When we started researching what you need to do to get a team to high performance, we identified several conditions for success, which we call the Edge Dynamics. Presented in a diamond, the Edge Dynamics (Reason, Results, Routines, Relationships and Resilience) interrelate with each other and are all equally critical for achieving and sustaining high performance. Focusing only on one or two just won't cut it. Your team will improve but they won't fulfil their potential, or they won't sustain high performance if they do achieve it. What we've found is that where you start with your team matters less than starting at all. If you work on one Edge Dynamic, you're working on others at the same time by default, but to really maximize the chances of achieving and then sustaining high performance, you need to work on all the Edge Dynamics over time. This book helps you to do that by exploring each of the Edge Dynamics, how their dynamic nature means that they impact each other and what you can do to develop them.

The Edge Dynamics are broad in nature on purpose – for example, it's not enough to focus on just Relationships between team members to achieve high performance. We've found that most other team models tend to focus on this or one other area alone and don't encompass everything that's needed to ensure success. We don't reject those models, they still have merit and purpose. In fact, if you have a favourite that you've referred to before, you'll still find a place for that in this book and our approach to teams. We would just suggest that there's more to high performance than any of those models would indicate.

Simplicity is key to high performance. If you want your team to engage in their own development, it needs to be anchored in a framework that's simple, memorable and powerful. We've based our whole approach (and this book) on those principles. In this book, you'll find an intuitive, easy to remember and impactful framework to support your team's performance edge.

High performance is by design

Any team can be a good team with a little bit of luck, a good leader and positive intentions from team members. However, it's impossible to be a high-performing team and sustain it indefinitely without putting effort into your team. A high-performing team is created by design and continuous focus on the conditions for success. This concept is well accepted in the sporting world. A high-performing sports team has continuous focus on the conditions for success in their context and have a plan, which they regularly review, to develop themselves as a team.

High performance isn't achieved through a one-off event – a team-building day can be fun but rarely has lasting impact and needs follow-up and follow-through to create change in the team. High performance is achieved through regular moments of focus on the team and their Edge Dynamics.

How to use this book

This book is designed to help you, as a leader, to unlock the potential of your team and take them to their performance edge (and beyond!). The book is in two parts. In Part One we explore the Edge Dynamics, which are the conditions for success in a high-performing team. We start with an overview of the principles and dynamics of high-performing teams (Chapter 1) and then we go deeper into each Edge Dynamic in turn (Chapters 2–6).

In Part Two we examine the development of both the leader and the team. In Chapter 7 we explore the behaviours you need as a leader to enable your team to achieve high performance. We follow this in Chapter 8 by discussing, with some insights from Formula 1, what gets in the way (interferences) and what will speed up your progress (accelerators) towards high performance. Finally, in Chapter 9 we explore some additional aspects that may impact team performance, such as team type and size, diversity and inclusion, cross-cultural teams and project and matrix teams.

Throughout the book you'll find helpful, short case studies with reference to tools and resources that you can use with your team – these can be downloaded free of charge on our website (www.management-dynamics.com/leading-edge). Each chapter also has a summary at the end that you can use as a powerful reference tool. If you ever need a quick reminder of the topics in the chapter, use this!

You don't need to read the chapters in consecutive order. It's written so that you can use it as a reference guide and dip in and out as you need to. If you were to start anywhere, we would suggest you read Chapter 1 first, then explore the chapters on the Edge Dynamics (Chapters 2–6) according to your level of interest. If you want to understand the role you play as a leader in your team, read Chapter 7 on leader behaviours.

Diamond Charter

Below you'll find what we call the 'Diamond Charter'. It's structured around each of the Edge Dynamics and the things a team needs to have in place to be effective. This is where you can bring together the outputs from the exercises and tools we reference in the book. Whenever you do an exercise with the team, you can capture a summary of it using the Diamond Charter. By completing it, you'll start to notice where the most significant gaps might lie in your team. It will help you to prioritize what to do with your team next. You can download a copy of this from our website.[6]

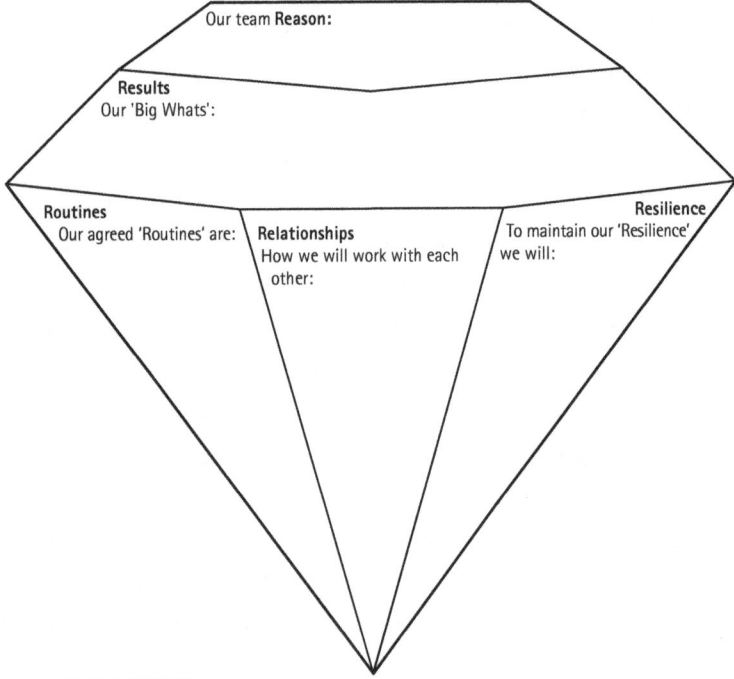

---

[6] www.management-dynamics.com/leading-edge

PART ONE
High-performing team dynamics

CHAPTER 1

The principles and dynamics of high-performing teams

In this chapter, we explore:

- The principles of high-performing teams – the things you as a leader and your team members need to pay attention to when considering how to get your team to high performance and sustain it.
- The Edge Dynamics – what they are, how they interact with each other and how to diagnose where your team is in relation to them.

The principles of high-performing teams

There are several principles to pay attention to as a leader when wanting to embark upon a journey to high performance with your team. These principles fall into two key categories: The first is all about your mindset as a leader and the second is about the team members' mindset. Your mindset is a set of beliefs that shape how you make sense of the world, yourself as a leader and others in the team. These beliefs influence how you think, feel and behave in the team. Leaders and team members need to be prepared to challenge both their ways of working and their thinking to take the team to the edge of their potential. This is how a high-performing team is created.

> *'If you believe that to be successful you first need to be a team, that's 90% of your journey.'*
>
> **David Allen**
> **Managing Director Pacific and Greater Asia, Pandora**

The leader's mindset

A leader's mindset is crucial in creating a high-performing team. If you as the team leader don't believe the team can get to high performance or, for whatever reason, you don't want them to, then there's no point in continuing. We've met many mediocre teams and leaders who are perfectly content and don't want high performance. They fear the effort they'll need to put in will be too great. If this is you, stop reading now. This book is not for you. If, however, you're ready to challenge your thinking, these are the things you'll need to embrace as a leader to pave the way for high performance in your team.

Shift your focus

Most leaders focus mainly on the individual team members in their team. This is the route to having a team made up of high-performing individuals, which sounds great, right? But there's something missing – having a bunch of high performers doesn't mean you have a high-performing team. Your high-performing individuals aren't getting the benefits of collaboration, synergy, interdependence and working together to achieve a common goal. How much more could your team members achieve if you harnessed the group's collaborative capability to solve complex problems and challenges facing them? Shift your focus as a leader from the team's individual members to the dynamics in the team as a whole as well. This will open up the potential for a high-performing team.

Know your place
As a leader of a team, you have a unique position within that team. You're a team member like everyone else, but one with a broader perspective of the team. You see the whole team from above as if from a helicopter. You interact regularly with all the team members. You also have an insight into the perspective of the team's other stakeholders (e.g. your bosses, peers, customers, other teams your team works with regularly) and the views they hold about your team.

Your role as leader is multifaceted. First of all, you're a guide to the team, helping them to focus and have clarity to head in the right direction and to work together to achieve their Results. You're also a member of the team in that you're also responsible for achieving the team's goals. But you're not doing it alone – you're doing it together with your team.

Give your team permission
Often, team members don't realize that they can feel a sense of ownership for the Results for their team. In the past they may have had only individual objectives and they also may not feel it's okay for them to get involved in other team members' work. Or they may feel they just don't have time for team objectives as well as their own. This is a very common problem and one that will hold your team back from ever achieving high performance. For this to change, you'll need to give everyone permission and make it clear to the team and every individual in it that they all have a responsibility

and accountability for the team as a whole as well as their own individual work.

Hold the team accountable
Once you've decided that you'd like to develop your team towards high performance, you need to give the team permission and then hold them accountable for helping you to create that. The responsibility for developing a high-performing team cannot rest on your shoulders alone as the leader of that team. Your team must be involved and accountable equally with you for creating it. Help your team members to understand what's in it for them personally from creating a high-performing team. Talk to the team regularly about a high-performing team and its benefits. Review the progress that they're making in moving towards high performance and celebrate the successes they're having.

Don't do it alone
If you've decided that you want to embark upon a high-performing team journey, you've given permission to your team and explained the benefits of high performance and they still aren't buying into it, do *not* continue. You'll achieve nothing. This isn't something that can be done 'to' a team. It's a do 'with' partnership process. Your team needs to be engaged and fully committed to developing the team in order for it to work. What's getting in the way? What are you doing as a leader that's enabling the team to stay stuck? What could you do differently to create a different outcome?

Create clarity
A big part of your role as a leader is to create clarity for your team. Clarity of expectations, clarity of purpose, clarity of

Results and how they're measured, clarity of behaviours, clarity of Routines and clarity of the way team members engage with each other. The greatest gift you can give your team as a leader is clarity, and your role is to constantly strive to ensure that everybody is clear on their own individual accountabilities and how those accountabilities align and connect with the team's accountabilities. It's also about ensuring that each team member understands what you expect from them and that they're accountable for the team's goals. Be clear on where you expect them to step up, take part and contribute, and help them understand where collaboration adds value.

Continuously focus on developing the team
Developing a team isn't a one-off event. It's not a one-day team-building session or a tick in the box exercise. It's a long-term, continuous focus on developing your team. You need to continue to invest in time together to learn where the challenges are, what's working well, to build even stronger Relationships, to maintain the team mindset and to learn from each other. A lot of teams get together every now and then to discuss the operational (the 'what') but don't invest in discussing the dynamics of the team (the 'how' and the 'why'). Ensure that you help your team to shift their focus from their own individual work to how they can achieve even more together as a team.

You can break the pattern
Some leaders tell us that they can't create a high-performing team because they themselves aren't part of one. They believe that to create a high-performing team the context in which that team is operating needs to be perfect. The reality is that it's never perfect. In our experience you can still create a

high-performing team even if the context is challenging for the team. In fact, you could argue that a challenging context makes developing your team to high performance even more important. In any case, you can still give the team the clarity that they need, and you can still shift their mindset towards high performance. You don't need to lead your team in the way that you're being led.

Don't settle for average
When you settle for average (or less) in your team, you're enabling a potential lack of motivation, lower engagement, the likelihood of losing your key people to other higher-performing teams and a general sense that things could be better. Is that okay? We would argue that there's more to be had than average (or less). What if your team was high-performing? What could you achieve together? How engaged and committed would your team members be? How much more engaged and committed would you be as a leader of that team? Imagine the Results and the impact that you and your team could have on the organization, your customers and each other if you and the team were high-performing.

Now is always a good time, even when it's not
Leaders tell us that it's not a good time to develop their team for one of two reasons. First of all, change is coming, so they want to wait until the team is stable and the change has been established in the team before developing them further. The second reason given is that they're overloaded with work and there's no time to develop their team at the moment. When things quieten down in a few months, they'd be delighted to focus on the team. The reality is that both of these reasons for not developing the team are actually compelling reasons

for getting started right now. There's never a time when you're not busy in a team. There's always change coming. There's always something critical on the horizon. Teams are dynamic and always shifting and, as we know, there's always going to be more work than you can ever handle – that's why you need to develop them as a team, to be ready when the critical moments hit or the change occurs. The team needs to anticipate changes and start to really connect and plan for how they work together going forward. Developing your team isn't an optional extra once everything else is perfect, it's part of the solution for dealing with change and high workloads. Let go of the excuses, start developing your team now.

Be self-aware

One of the first places to start when embarking on a process to develop your team is with yourself. Start to notice the impact you're having on your team – is it a positive one? Are you helping them to get to high performance, or are you getting in their way? This can be a tough thing to consider, especially when you start to realize that a leader will always get in their team's way somewhere! Accept this and start to work on how to minimize the negative impacts you have and maximize the positive ones. We've dedicated a whole chapter to this (see Chapter 7 'Leading a high-performing team') so that you can explore it further.

Team members' mindset

In an average team, team members focus more on their own individual work than they do on the team. This is a very limiting mindset and the team will only achieve so much with it in place. It's essential, as a leader, to shift your team's mindset from 'me' to 'we' – from 'me' as an individual with my own objectives and focus, to 'we' as a team and what we can achieve together. When this mindset shifts, team members focus on collaboration, sharing best practices, learning from each other, working on things together, brainstorming ideas and challenging each other to make better decisions. All of these things come out of two critical mindsets:

- The team's work is as important as my own individual work.
- I'm accountable and responsible for the whole team as much as my leader is.

Here are some other key things that your team needs to pay attention to so that they can achieve and maintain high performance.

Buy in to high performance
A big objection to high performance can be that it means high workloads – even higher workloads than team members already have. We know that's just not the case, so your role as leader is to help people to understand that high performance means working smarter not harder. It means helping them to understand that there are massive benefits to them as individuals to working together as a team. That they can achieve so much more together than they could possibly hope to achieve on their own. That work will be easier and more enjoyable when they collaborate on tasks as a team. That there will be more opportunities for personal growth and support as part of a high-performing team. That the opportunity to create high levels of Resilience is far greater when they have other people supporting them.

Be accountable

It's not just a leader's role to hold the team accountable. In high-performing teams, what we see is team members holding each other accountable for key tasks, decisions made as a team, outputs and expected behaviours. Instead of going to the leader to escalate issues with another team member, they'll go directly to the relevant team member themselves and discuss it together. Team members will make decisions themselves rather than feeling they have to push everything up to the leader. They feel accountable and empowered to make those decisions and know that the rest of the team will stand by them and commit to those decisions.

Be a radar

Once your team has bought into and is accountable for creating high performance, you need them to be constantly on the lookout for changes. Shifts in the context in which they're working; new information that may be of interest either to themselves or other team members; new ways of working that could improve the team's efficiency and any other potential opportunities that could be of benefit to other individuals or the team as a whole. Every team member needs to operate like the team's radar system, scanning continuously and sharing with the rest of the team.

Be courageous

Developing a team to high performance isn't easy – it takes time, effort and courage to take the team and yourself to the edge and beyond. It takes courage for the team to step out of their comfort zone. Courage for team members to show vulnerability and to speak out about things they might not be 100% sure of but that could be of value to the team. Courage to step up and be brave and to create an environment of safety where everybody knows that the team is having a go. All of this is stretching towards the edge, which might be a bit challenging for the team, but so worth it.

Team development is an ongoing practice

Many of the existing tools and practices around teams focus on the team in one moment in time and we would argue that team development should be more like an ongoing practice towards high performance. Teams aren't static. Teams are adjusting and shifting all the time, they're dynamic. Teams are always changing – the people in the team change, the context in which the team is working changes, the organization changes, their customers and stakeholders' expectations change and the processes and rhythms they work with change. This creates complexity within a team, which requires continuous focus and attention.

Overview of the Edge Dynamics

When we first started thinking about high performance, we found there were over 5,000 research papers on teams, all with different perspectives. So, we decided to narrow down our focus to what was critical for the success of not just any team, but a high-performing one. What gives a high-performing team an edge? We really wanted to differentiate between a good and a high-performing team. From this, we distilled the research into the core factors of high-performing teams, which we call the Edge Dynamics.

The principles and dynamics of high-performing teams

The Edge Dynamics

The Edge Dynamics are Reason, Results, Routines, Relationships and Resilience. Together these Edge Dynamics interact and support each other to create a sustainable high-performing team. The framework is simple without being simplistic. It's a practical, intuitive methodology for you and your team to work with so that you can take your team to the edge of their potential and beyond.

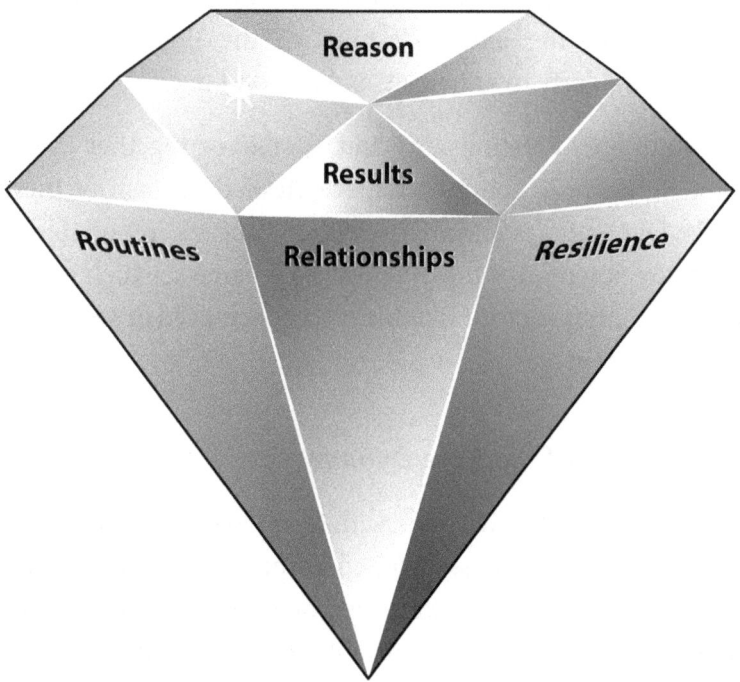

- Reason – the team's *why*. Without it the team has no purpose – nothing to guide it towards where it needs to go.
- Results – *what* the team is accountable for delivering together. Without this, there can be duplication of

effort and, at best, mediocre performance with an individual focus in a team.
- Routines – the team's ways of working, its rhythms, how the team members keep each other informed and make decisions.
- Relationships – what it feels like to be a part of this team and how team members work with and interact with each other.
- Resilience – the energy levels of the team, learning from experiences to continuously improve and reviewing and refreshing all the Edge Dynamics regularly to anticipate and respond to changes.

Routines, Relationships and Resilience together create *how* the team is going to achieve all of this. Each of these Edge Dynamics is essential – without one it's impossible to fulfil the potential of the other Edge Dynamics, which means that high performance is unlikely to be achieved or very difficult to sustain.

Work on all of the Edge Dynamics

Through our extensive work with teams, we found that many of them have previously worked on one or two of the Edge Dynamics, such as Relationships or Routines, and yet they were missing the most important piece of the puzzle, which is that a team needs to work on all of the Edge Dynamics to get to high performance. You'll definitely improve the performance of your team by working on one or two Edge Dynamics, but to really get to that high performance and to sustain it over time, you need to harness all of the Edge

Dynamics *together*. This is because they work in an integrated way, supporting each other.

The diamond analogy

We use the analogy of a diamond when we talk about high-performing teams. We all know how special and valuable a diamond is, and when we talk to leaders they know implicitly how special and valuable a high-performing team is. Diamonds are multifaceted – when you look at them, they look different, depending on the angle and context that they're in. Teams also change depending on their context and are made up of different people, which also makes them multifaceted. High-performing teams, like diamonds, are hard to find, and once you have one, you'll want to maintain it and sustain that high performance and the value that it brings to you as a leader and your organization. It takes a long time to mine, cut and polish a diamond, and to fulfil the potential value of the diamond you need to go through the full process. A high-performing team takes time and effort to form, develop and sustain to fulfil its full potential. The team needs to establish strong foundations in all of the Edge Dynamics to make this happen. The *why, what* and *how* need to be established and revisited regularly to polish your diamond. A diamond is the strongest natural material, used on the tips of drills to cut through pretty much anything. A high-performing team should be like a diamond, resilient and focused enough to cut through anything together. Finally, and probably most importantly, it takes a diamond to cut another diamond, and as a leader you need to be high-performing yourself to create a high-performing team.

Diagnosing your team

One of the most challenging aspects of team development is knowing what to focus on with your team at any given time. Teams are complex systems and there are so many different areas that you could work on. But how do you know where to start and what will make the difference for your team right now? The only way to know where to focus is to do some kind of diagnosis of your team against the Edge Dynamics of high-performing teams. So, we've created a diagnostic tool to help you with this (see section on 'Accessing the diagnostic tool' later in this chapter). The tool will help you to identify where you'll get the greatest value from your efforts and which Edge Dynamic/s will give you the best return on your investment in moving towards high performance.

Why bother with diagnosing your team?

So why bother diagnosing your team? Well, there are three key things that are compelling reasons for doing a regular diagnostic of the Edge Dynamics. A diagnostic helps to make something that's rather subjective (in other words how it feels to be a part of this team) into something much more tangible and data-driven. Without a diagnostic, you're working with people's opinions and the danger is that the loudest voice in the room is the one that's heard, while other voices get silenced. It can be hard to establish what the team as a whole really thinks. Using a research-based, anonymous diagnostic linked to what really impacts performance as a team, enables you to focus and be confident that what you're working on will deliver and support the team in their objectives.

Regular diagnostics are key

Don't stop there though! Once you've taken some action for your team, we would suggest you use your chosen diagnostic tool regularly to measure and review progress. As already mentioned, it's an ongoing practice to get to high performance and to sustain it. The team is constantly shifting and adjusting and you need to know what has changed so that you can adapt to it. Regular diagnostics will also help you celebrate successes and see the progress your team is making against the Edge Dynamics and to diagnose and identify what you should focus on next. We would recommend using a diagnostic tool roughly every three months with your team. This is a good rhythm to create to check in with your team on how things are going against the Edge Dynamics. It also keeps pace with any changes and shifts that are going on in the general context.

The first diagnostic

The first diagnostic that you do will give you a baseline for your team. Where's your team right now against each of the Edge Dynamics and what should the priority be for your team? Diagnosing your team also helps you to prioritize the action that you and your team take in developing your team towards high performance. There are lots of factors that contribute to high performance in teams and every team is different, so knowing where to start is crucial, otherwise you and the team can get overwhelmed very easily and achieve little.

How often?

Doing a diagnostic every three months or as regularly as possible also enables you to track the progress that the team is making against the Edge Dynamics of high-performing teams. It's useful to be able to see where you're making the greatest difference as a team, where the gaps still lie and where you should focus your attention as a team in the future. It also provides a barometer to review how changes impact the team so you can take immediate action or anticipate action before those changes have an effect on the performance of the team. As Karl Pearson said, 'When performance is measured, performance improves. When performance is measured and reported back, the rate of improvement accelerates.'[7]

Accessing the diagnostic tool

There are three options for accessing the diagnostic tool that measures the Edge Dynamics of high-performing teams.

Comprehensive diagnostic assessment for the team

The first option is to buy a subscription to our cloud-based, research-powered solution, Advantycs®, which you can learn more about on our website.[8] This solution enables the leader and the team to provide their assessment of the team against 25 questions and Stop, Start, Continue comments. The results are presented against each of the Edge Dynamics in a downloadable report. The assessment is anonymous for the team

---

[7] https://positioningsystems.com/blog.php?entryID=67
[8] www.management-dynamics.com/leading-edge

members to complete. The team can then discuss and use the results to take action and track their progress over time.

Leader-only assessment

We've created a 'leader-only' version of the diagnostic tool,[9] which is free to access and enables you to answer 25 questions about your team and see the consolidated results in a report. It provides the same research-based diagnostic described above but is answered by just you as the leader of the team. This will give you a flavour of where your team is and will help you prioritize where you think the team should start.

Diagnostic coaching questions

The third option is to carry out a more informal diagnosis using the coaching questions you'll find below. There are a couple of different ways you could use them:

- Firstly, spend some time considering the questions by yourself and think about what you could do with the team to develop the gaps the diagnostic identifies.
- Secondly, (and always our preference) would be to discuss the diagnostic coaching questions with your team. This gets the full team involved in diagnosing their current status as a team and creates buy-in for the process from them, which as we've already established is crucial.

The questions are:

- How clear is your team on what the team's purpose is?

---

[9] www.management-dynamics.com/leading-edge

- How do team members articulate the team's purpose to others?
- What's your team accountable for delivering?
- How clear is your team on the team's accountabilities?
- What are Relationships like in your team?
- To what extent is constructive challenge a habit in your team?
- How well do the team's Routines serve the team right now?
- Who makes most of the decisions in your team?
- How does your team anticipate changes that affect the team?
- How are your team members' energy levels right now?

How the Edge Dynamics interact with each other

It's worth spending some time exploring how the Edge Dynamics interact with each other and there's no strong set process for how to engage with them. Consider what your team needs right now.

Where do you start?

People often ask us, 'Where do I start when developing my team? Which Dynamic has priority?' There's a broad sequence and a rule of thumb to follow when developing your team, which is to start with Reason: understand the team's *why*, then get clarity on the team's Results and explore the *how*, including the Relationships, the Routines and Resilience in the team.

However, the reality is that *all* of the Edge Dynamics are deeply interconnected with each other. Edge Dynamics are levers you can pull as a leader to have an impact on your team, and by focusing on one Edge Dynamic you'll naturally, by extension, impact other Edge Dynamics at the same time.

Lack of connection to Reason

What we've noticed, working with hundreds of teams, is that if a team is overworked it can be easy to lose sight of their Reason. Reminding and reconnecting teams of their Reason – their why – can really help them to focus and re-energize to move forward.

Poor Relationships

We've also noticed that if Relationships aren't working in a team, then it's really hard to deliver on Results in that team – the team gets distracted by conflict, opinions and ideas aren't shared and poor decisions are made. If a team's Routines are out of date or cumbersome, this can damage both the Relationships within the team and their ability to deliver on Results. It also leaves the team feeling demotivated and disengaged, which impacts Resilience.

When Relationships are poor in a team, what we often find is that certain team members can be excluded from the team process. So, for example, in a team meeting, their opinions are shut down or they're not invited to share their opinions in the first place. This will impact Relationships within the team but also the Results that the team can potentially achieve. Results will be limited by the lack of diversity of thought, debate and challenge within the team. The team may also be a victim of 'group think'.

Low Resilience

When Resilience is low in a team, getting clarity on the Reason and the Results impacts the Resilience of the team as they're now able to see the wood for the trees, to be able to prioritize and to focus on building Relationships within the team to get stuff done. Ultimately, it doesn't really matter where you start. What's more important is actually starting and getting your team's buy-in to doing so. Work with your team to decide where they'd like to start first and which Edge Dynamics would make the most sense for you and your team right now.

> **Team case study**
>
> This team comprised nine team members. They'd just gone through a huge transformation and 90% of the team were new. The leader had only been in place for six months. The team members were all deep experts in their field, high performers, with a track record of individual high achievement and delivery. The team members were all nice people with ambition – as long as everyone let them get on with their work! The leader had very ambitious plans for the team Results, and expectations from the organization were high.
>
> When we first started working with the team, we ran their first diagnostic. Scores were very low across the board, with the exception of Reason, which was okay. In the comments, team members complained of high workloads, duplication of effort, competing commitments and a lack of a sense of team. They were clearly very siloed and almost competing with each other, rather than a real team at this stage.

The team identified that they'd like to start with Reason and Results to ensure that the clarity of the team's *why* and *what* were nailed early on. Having gone through the process, they realized that collaboration was an essential part of delivering their Results and that their *why* was the glue that held them together – they all wanted more than just the delivery of some KPIs, they wanted to make a difference to their organization and leave a legacy. They also wanted to grow as leaders themselves in the process.

We spent time working with them to align team members to the Reason. When we first started working with them, each team member articulated the team Reason differently. By the time we had finished, they had one compelling team Reason, which everyone was aligned and connected to. This enabled them to prioritize the Results of the team to reduce them from 63 KPIs down to five key KPIs for the team as a whole. They identified their 'Big Whats' (the key things that the team was accountable for delivering together) and they knew how to measure and report on them to each other and the wider business. They identified where to collaborate with each other to achieve these 'Big Whats' (see Chapter 3), so now, rather than competing with each other to get their project across the line, they were now using their resources more wisely and working together to achieve a common aim. They also changed their Routines to create new ones and adjust their existing ones to enable all the other Edge Dynamics to flourish.

When we re-ran the diagnostic a few months later, not only had the scores for Reason and Results improved (as we had hoped!) and were now high, but Relationships, Routines and Resilience were now better too, although they still had some way to go. The impact on the business was immediate. Their direct reports noticed the knock-on effects of the clarity they created in the leadership team. They themselves were now able to prioritize work in line with the 'Big Whats'. They also started to collaborate more across teams within the function and feel a sense of purpose in their work. The team's stakeholders also started to notice a difference. They experienced better communication and clarity about what was being delivered and the connections between what they were delivering and the overall business strategy. They could see that there was room for improvement still, but it was definitely heading in the right direction.

The next thing that the team prioritized in terms of team development was Relationships. Now that they were clear on the *why* and the *what*, the focus shifted to the *how*. A key issue in the team was a lack of trust and understanding of very different types of people. This was a hugely diverse group made up of different nationalities and backgrounds, with plenty of room for misunderstandings. There was also a variation of personalities across the team, with some preferring to focus on the task and others preferring Relationships first. A lot of their Relationships had been formed during COVID-19, which meant they were superficial and transactional in nature.

We spent time with the team helping them to get to know each other better and at a deeper level, going beyond the basic level of trust to more of a vulnerability-based trust (which is essential in a high-performing team). They shared their motivations and what was maximizing or hindering their effectiveness with each other. They gave each other feedback in a way that helped them express what they appreciated in others and what they'd like others to change.

A third diagnostic showed what we had hoped for, an increase in the scores on Relationships, but also an increase in all the other Edge Dynamics. Still there was work to do, but the team Edge Dynamics were heading in the right direction. The team members were now collaborating much more and were enjoying working together and being included in delivering team accountabilities.

Team development is an ongoing process, one that happens incrementally over time. The process so far has taken the team nine months and, in that time, they saw a 35% increase in their diagnostic scores overall. They're still ambitious for more, but they're already seeing a marked difference in both achievement of team KPIs and how it feels to be a part of this team. One particular KPI that had previously stalled due to a lack of collaboration and ownership, was achieved with great Results.

The principles and dynamics of high-performing teams – a summary

To embark upon a high-performing team process with your team, you must consider:

- Your own mindset as leader
- The mindset of your team

Team development is an ongoing practice. You won't get a high-performing team overnight. It takes deliberate action by the whole team.

The Edge Dynamics of high-performing teams are:

- Reason
- Results
- Routines
- Relationships
- Resilience

Reason is *why* the team exists, its purpose beyond delivering KPIs.

Results are *what* the team is accountable for delivering.

Routines, Relationships and Resilience are *how* the team operates.

All of the Edge Dynamics interact with and impact each other, so you'll need to pay attention to and work on all of them to achieve high performance. Use a diagnostic tool, such as Advantycs®, regularly to determine how your team is doing against each of the Edge Dynamics.

CHAPTER 2

Reason

Get really clear about the team's purpose and value to the organization as well as individual team members' connections to that Reason. This is the team's Reason for being and the starting point for everything.

What is Reason?

Reason is the team's *why*. It's their North Star, which provides direction to the team when they need it most. It's the Reason *why* the team was created in the first place and a sense of the value the team brings to the organization and its customers. The organization will have created a design for your team and made some decisions about how the team is set up, its place in the organization and their expected outcomes and impact. They had a choice to set it up differently or to expect different outcomes. What is it that led to this particular mix of people, group of skills and knowledge? The team's Reason is aspirational, values and principles-based and, most importantly, it needs to be enduring and connect with everyone in the team in some way.

When we talk to leaders, they often mix up Reason and Results. They often think that *what* the team is expected to deliver (in other words their KPIs/objectives/goals) is the Reason they exist. But it's so much more than that. Results are important to a team, but to be truly motivated and fulfilled, teams need a more compelling Reason than just achieving their objectives. A Reason lasts a lot longer than the team's KPIs.

The *why* is harder to create than the *what* because it's much deeper and more impactful for team members. We need to ask ourselves a lot more questions to create it. Often assumptions are made, or the Reason is created in isolation of the team. The best team Reasons include the team in their creation in some way.

Why is Reason important?

A team Reason might sound a bit soft and fluffy, and our guess is that if your team doesn't have one already, you might not really see the value in having a defined team Reason. But there's a compelling business case for having one – in fact, according to McKinsey, 'There is a 1.9 times increased likelihood of having above-median financial performance when the top team is working together toward a common vision.'[10] If it works for a top team, it by extension must be important for any team to have a clear vision, a clear Reason for their existence.

People are more motivated when they have a strong *why*. That's why Reason is more than just a completion of a task or achieving a KPI. Team members need to understand the impact of the work that they're doing and that their work has meaning or contributes to the organization and its customers in some way. This contribution and meaning are what motivate people intrinsically. People also need to feel that the contribution they're making is bigger than just making money for some faceless shareholders. We hear a lot

---

[10] www.mckinsey.com/business-functions/people-and-organizational-performance/our-insights/high-performing-teams-a-timeless-leadership-topic

of organizations talk about adding shareholder value or value creation, but that's not enough to motivate team members by itself. In any case, even shareholders themselves now want more ethical investments and are demanding to know that there's a sustainable approach to their return on investment.

We've already mentioned that the Reason is your team's North Star. The Reason helps you as a team to make decisions on whether what you're doing will help you achieve your *why*. It helps you to prioritize your Results and the things that really matter. Without a *why* you're leaving your team's motivation up to chance and you may be missing an opportunity to really engage your team members at a deeper level. Reason has always been important, but we notice it even more with new Generation Z employees entering the workforce, for whom '42% would rather be at a company with a sense of purpose, rather than one that pays more'.[11]

'A strong purpose is needed in a crisis or rapidly changing circumstances. It is when it is determined whether it is really a purpose or whether it is just a statement.'

**Frederic Debrosses
General Manager Middle East, Africa,
Global Business Development, JDE Peet's**

When we look at the neuroscience of motivation, we find that when you think about *what* you do at work, your neocortex (in other words, your thinking brain) is triggered, it lights up – but this is not where motivation lies, just

---

[11] www.forbes.com/sites/barnabylashbrooke/2022/08/24/its-time-to-retire-lazy-generalizations-about-gen-z-in-the-workplace/?sh=3f74d5b5afe3

satisfaction. When we think about *why* we do something, our limbic system (in other words, your feeling brain) is triggered and lights up – this is where true motivation, passion, dedication and fulfilment lie. If you want someone to feel really motivated, you have to light up their limbic system. This comes from the *why*.

The impact of Reason on team performance

Having a compelling Reason results in a positive impact on your team's performance. Without it, team members can feel like the relentless Results focus is never-ending. It can feel like their only purpose is to deliver short-term KPI-driven goals. And where's the fulfilment in that?

A compelling Reason connects team members to others in the team with a shared common purpose. It also taps into team members' intrinsic motivations and gives them a sense of pride in the team's impact. This will get them out of bed in the morning and help them to enjoy their work every day.

We know, from research, that when people are motivated they go the extra mile. They give discretionary effort and energy, which means that their output is superior. This doesn't mean that they work longer hours (which, let's face it, is often unsustainable anyway) but they'll definitely work smarter and collaborate more effectively with others. Working in this way re-energizes and refreshes the team and is ultimately much more rewarding for them (and, by extension, you as their leader). It also enables them to tap into their creativity and innovation more easily, as they take in a broader context.

The four levels of Reason

There are four levels of Reason: individual, team, organization and society. Let's look at each in turn.

Individual

Each of us has a Reason why we come to work each day – our own personal purpose. You might call this your values or your motives and it's very personal to each of us. People are like icebergs: 90% of an iceberg is under water, so, in our case, 90% of us is hidden, not seen by others. The bit above the surface that people see of us is our behaviour – how we do things on a day-to-day basis. And that behaviour might change in different contexts. Under the surface of the water, what people don't see are our motivations, our values and our beliefs. These things drive our behaviour. This is *why* we do things. For example, Jenni has a value for making a difference. It's her most important value at work. She seeks out opportunities every day to make a difference to the people, teams and organizations that she works with. She's at her most motivated when this value is being fulfilled. She also notices that she can get demotivated when that value isn't being fulfilled. For example, if she has to spend too long doing a tax return or company admin, she can notice a drop in her personal motivation.

Our values are the things that we're often prepared to stand up and fight for. They can therefore be the source of conflict in a team if team members don't respect other people's values.

It's amazing what a difference it can make in a team when people share and understand each other's values, and it's easy to talk about them, as they just *are*. People are often surprised how rarely money appears in their values. If it is there, it's usually about what money means to them, like contribution or security or abundance, rather than just money itself. And that's because money can be a big demotivator if it's not present but is usually not a motivator in and of itself.

It's useful to share your personal values with your team to enable your team members to help you to fulfil them. For example, one of our team members really values connection. To him this means working face to face with others regularly and really spending time with other people. We notice as a team when he hasn't had the opportunity to do this; it affects his motivation. We also notice the impact on his work when he does have the opportunity to connect with others. He's more energized, articulate and passionate about his work. This is when the ideas really flow for him. As a team, we can easily support him to fulfil this value by giving him opportunities to connect with us, with clients and suppliers regularly.

As a team, it's also useful to notice the similarities and differences in each other's values. People might name their values differently (e.g. respect and integrity) and yet, when you hear them describe what those values mean to them, you can see that there are some very similar themes. Similarity is important for bringing a team together and showing that they're connected to each other. In the same way, differences enrich the team and bring different perspectives and thinking to them. Problems can be solved more easily, in diverse ways.

When values aren't fulfilled in a team or are compromised in some way, team members can be very disengaged and demotivated. At worst, they may even leave the team. We'll often help a team to explore what would cause each team member to leave that team. In our experience of working with lots of teams on their values, it's usually linked to one of their most important work values and many team members will describe times when they've left a team because that value has been unfulfilled.

When conflict occurs in a team, invariably it's due to a value being 'stepped on' or challenged in some way. For example, a team member might accuse a colleague of treating them unfairly, and if fairness is an important value for the colleague being accused, fireworks can follow! Understanding each other's values helps team members appreciate why a conflict has occurred and enables them to adjust their language, apologize if necessary and move forward from the conflict.

Team

Team Reason is about understanding and getting really clear on *why* your team exists. Why is this team a team and not just a bunch of people who happen to work for the same boss?

What's the contribution they're aspiring to make together? What's bigger than just delivering a certain number of widgets or making a certain amount of money for the business? This is your team's *why* and is what will keep the team going even when the going gets tough.

Here are some examples of a few team Reasons:

- Delivering tomorrow, today (a transformation team)
- Deliver… together (a logistics teams)
- Catalysing world-class performance (our team)

We find that teams really love their Reason once they've got it, as long it meets the criterion of brief, memorable and inspirational (BMI). Brief enough that it's memorable to team members and it just rolls off the tongue. Inspiring means that it connects with each person in some way and ticks off one or more of their values.

A team Reason is not for others and it's not a marketing exercise – the team Reason is just for the team, at least initially. It's about articulating something in such a way that it galvanizes the team towards a compelling purpose. We'll talk a bit later about some ideas for how you could create a Reason for your team.

Organization

We then have the organizational Reason, the Reason the organization exists – again, this is more than just about making money, or 'creating shareholder value' as it's sometimes known. Often called a mission, vision or purpose, Reasons are articulated by many organizations in different ways, and the best ones, in our opinion, meet that BMI criterion as well.

Here are some examples:

- 'Spread ideas' – TED Talks
- 'To accelerate the world's transition to sustainable energy' – Tesla
- 'To inspire and nurture the human spirit, one person, one cup and one neighbourhood at a time' – Starbucks

Society

An organization doesn't exist in a vacuum, and every organization has an impact, positive or negative, on society and on the world around it, of which it's a part. So societal impacts are important to pay attention to. There are so many things that different cultures value and place importance upon, and here are just a few that are part of the global consciousness right now:

- *Climate change* – how are organizations affecting this? Are they behaving responsibly and making a difference, no matter how small? Or are they just ignoring or even exacerbating the problem?
- *Connection* – how do human beings connect with each other? Are they treating people well? Are they supporting connection between people?
- *Inclusion* – how inclusive a culture does the organization have? How inclusive are they with their customers?

Just a few thoughts, but these are the things an individual team member will be paying attention to, even subconsciously, and this will be impacting their own motivation and willingness to go the extra mile for the organization and the team.

Alignment of the four levels

These four levels aren't isolated from each other, they're all interdependent and therefore need to be aligned to help you realize the true power of Reason in your team.

```
┌─────────────────┐
│     Society     │
└─────────────────┘
         ↑
┌─────────────────┐
│  Organization   │
└─────────────────┘
         ↑
┌─────────────────┐
│      Team       │
└─────────────────┘
         ↑
┌─────────────────┐
│   Individual    │
└─────────────────┘
```

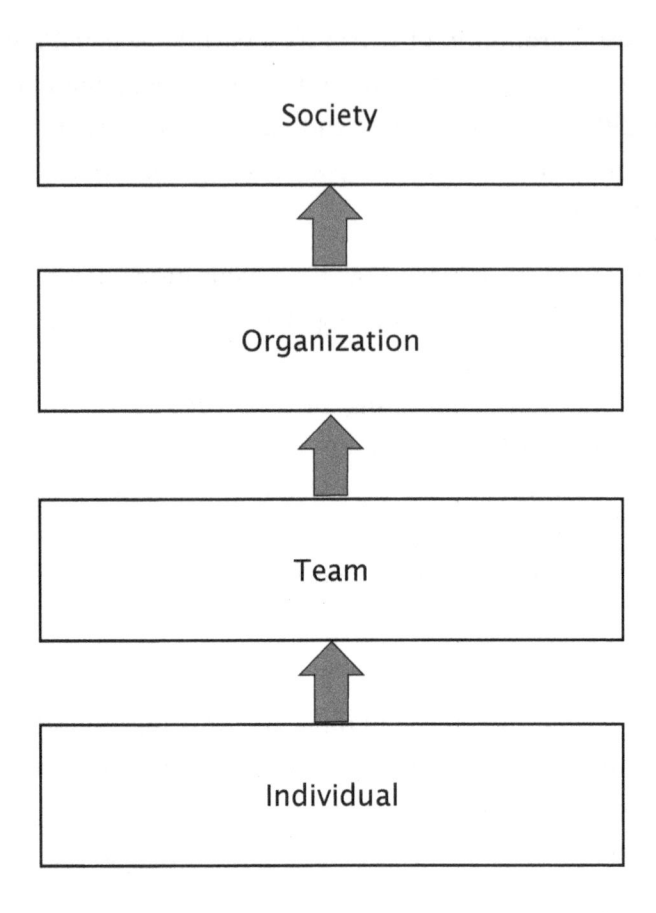

An individual in a team needs to feel personally motivated and understand what they need to be really motivated and how that can be fulfilled by the team. The team needs to have a compelling Reason for its existence, which the team all need to be connected to in some way. This, in turn, needs to be linked to the organizational mission, which, in turn, needs to impact society positively.

Think about how you can help your team members to make that connection for themselves without leaving it up to chance. If your organization doesn't have a mission or has minimal positive societal impact, don't give up – start with your team and its team Reason, and help team members connect to that.

Creating a team Reason

So how do you go about creating a team Reason? Well, the first thing to say is that this isn't necessarily a straightforward process and it depends a lot on the personalities of the team members involved as to whether they'll find this easy or not.

We worked with a team recently who had spent six hours already trying to create their team purpose. They got stuck, so called us in to help. We quickly realized they'd been working on their *what*, not their *why*. So, of course, no one was getting particularly inspired by it. Once we shifted the focus to their *why*, it became so much easier. They'd been trying to describe what the team did in an inspirational way and it's really hard to find inspiration in a list of day-to-day tasks. It's like us trying to find inspiration in *what* we do: 'we coach teams'. That's not particularly motivating or engaging, is it? It's *what* we do, but it's not going to ignite our team members' passion or excitement in any way. If we focus on our *why*, it all changes. Our *why* is: 'catalysing world-class performance'. What a difference. This is inspirational and every team member can connect to it in some way, no matter what their role is.

Then, we also set the scene by saying that the purpose needs to be BMI. We'll often start with a bottom-up approach – with what's important to individual team members. We kick-off with the team members sharing their individual Reason/values with each other and then doing group work to brainstorm a team Reason together.

Another option is to start with what the team wants to be known for or how they want their customers/stakeholders to feel, then brainstorming the team Reason from there. Both of these approaches ensure that the team Reason is anchored in team members' motivations.

It can be an iterative process, with teams coming up with something, sitting with it for a few days/weeks, then refining it.

How Reason changes when the team changes

A team Reason can be quite enduring, but every now and then might need a refresh, especially if the team context or composition has changed significantly, such as a new leader starting in the team, a transformation, a significant number of team members joining or leaving the team, etc. The key thing is to keep it alive and keep talking about it. Otherwise, it becomes another tick-box exercise with little meaning.

Our first team Reason was 'Inspiring growth every day', which worked well for the team at the time. We created it by getting our core team to define and share work values with the rest of the team. In two small groups, we then used those values to come up with a couple of sentences that described a Reason the whole team could connect to. As a whole group, we then compared and discussed the two sentences and ended up merging and refining until we were all happy with the final sentence of 'Inspiring growth every day'. Four years later, our business and our team members had shifted and changed dramatically, so this Reason no longer engaged us as it once used to. So, we did the exercise again and out came, 'Catalysing world-class performance'. This linked nicely to our desire for data-driven team and leadership development and the idea that we're the spark that ignites performance in our client organizations, in ourselves as individuals and as a team.

When you have new team members joining, you need to integrate them into the team. This means inducting them to the team's Reason. A new team member joining doesn't mean that you need to assimilate them into the team – they don't need to become like everybody else. However, it's an opportunity for the team to reassess their Reason and to realign everybody's motivations with the *why* of the team. We've seen a team create a word cloud of their values, which was very visual and a great tool for the team to use to remind themselves of their shared values. Whenever a team member leaves and a new person joins the team, the team members go through a process of sharing their values with the new member, hearing that person's values too and creating an updated word cloud for the team values.

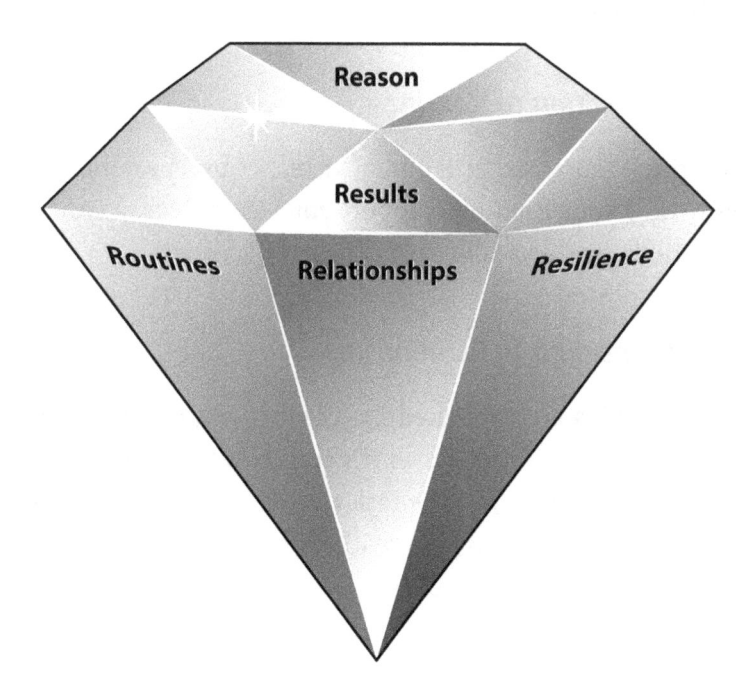

The links to other Edge Dynamics

Reason is perhaps the most fundamental Edge Dynamic and holds all the other Edge Dynamics together. It's like your team's North Star, and without it your team is directionless and solely task-focused. When a team has a clear Reason, it has strong motivation, which will keep you going as a team when times are tough and ambiguous. It does this in a way that no other Edge Dynamic can. When your Reason is clear, all the other Edge Dynamics become easier to establish and improve.

The connection to Results

Just like Reason, Results is about clarity. However, Results on their own are very functional, operational and, let's face it, possibly boring! The team's Reason brings life and purpose to their Results.

The connection to Routines

Routines can easily get out of date, so by checking regularly how your Routines support your team Reason, you can ensure they're always fit for purpose.

The connection to Relationships

Relationships are deepened by a team Reason. The Reason creates a shared purpose, which connects team members to each other beyond just the task they're doing. It encourages collaboration for a purpose that's higher than just delivery of a KPI.

The connection to Resilience

Resilience relies on a strong team Reason, as it provides motivation for the team to keep on going even when the going gets tough. It enables the team to bounce forwards after setbacks, as it focuses the team on their Reason even when 'failures' happen. When a team has a clear Reason they can more easily re-energize and self-motivate towards their purpose. They support each other more readily when energy is low, and their shared purpose glues them together as a team.

> **Reason – a summary**
>
> Reason is the team's *why*. It's their North Star, which provides direction to the team when they need it most. It's the Reason why the team was created in the first place and a sense of the value the team brings to the organization and its customers.
>
> People are motivated when they have a strong *why*. Team members need to understand the impact of the work that they're doing and that their work has meaning or contributes to the organization and its customers in some way.
>
> A compelling Reason connects team members to others in the team with a shared common purpose.
>
> There are four levels of Reason:
>
> - Individual
> - Team
> - Organization
> - Society

These four levels are all interdependent and therefore need to be aligned to help you realize the true power of Reason in your team.

Make sure that your team Reason is:

- Brief
- Memorable
- Inspiring

Keep your team Reason alive by talking about it with the team regularly. It may need a refresh when significant changes affect the team.

CHAPTER 3

Results

Get absolute clarity about what your team is accountable for delivering, in a way that's easily memorable and visible for the whole team. Align everyone's objectives and share that with the team. Encourage teamworking across shared deliverables.

What do we mean by Results?

When we talk to leaders, initially they'll tell us that Results is the Edge Dynamic they need to work on the least. Leaders frequently score Results higher than their team members do on our diagnostic. This is because there's often a strong focus in organizations on KPIs/objectives, goals/targets. There's also an assumption that because people know what to do in their job, they're clear on what Results are required at the team level. However, this strong focus on objectives and targets in organizations often results in teams having vast numbers of KPIs to achieve. This leads to a lack of clarity at the team level and also at the individual level around what this team is ultimately accountable for delivering. It also leads to an inability to prioritize well and to focus on the activities that will make the biggest difference to the organization as a whole. Consider the 80/20 rule; what are the 20% of accountabilities that will add the 80% of value to the team and the organization?[12] Less is more when it comes to team accountabilities.

We also find that there's a real lack of measurement of goals and objectives in organizations, particularly at the team level. Organizations are generally okay at making sure everybody has personal work objectives, but they're often considerably lacking when it comes to making sure those individuals can measure their objectives and, when we get to the team level, measurable team objectives are usually non-existent.

Clarity: the biggest gift you can give your team

One of the biggest gifts that you can give your team is clarity, and clarity on Results is essential for a high-performing team. Without it, team members are almost guaranteed to be working on their own tasks without involving others. We find that they might well be working at odds or cutting across the work of other team members. In fact, in the teams with the greatest lack of clarity around Results, they're often competing and maybe even undermining the work of others in the team. This causes huge frustration, creates conflict and destroys Relationships in teams. So, you can see how essential clarity of Results is in a team.

A lack of clarity is a key root cause of overload and overwhelm in a team. Overload eventually leads to demotivation and ineffective work practices, which then leads to absence and people leaving the team. Overload occurs in teams because people don't know how to prioritize

---

[12] https://en.wikipedia.org/wiki/Pareto_principle

or push back on unnecessary requests. When they have clarity on the key things that the team is accountable for delivering, they're much better placed to be able to prioritize their work, push back on things that add less value and focus on the things that make the biggest difference to the organization.

Once you have clarity of Results as a team, it's important to keep reinforcing it, circling back to ensure that everyone is still clear, despite new information. It's also important to refresh your Results regularly as the organizational strategy shifts or the expectations on the team change.

You'll need to create Routines (see Chapter 4) around how you measure and report on your Results as a team. How will you keep focus on your Results? How will you know it's time to adjust them? How do you bring new people on board to your Results? How do you adjust the team's workloads in times of absence or a lack of resource?

Alignment of Results

Just like with Reason, Results has different aspects that you need to pay attention to as a leader. Team members of course need individual objectives and KPIs and these are usually expected within an organization. Performance management processes usually measure and reward individual achievement of objectives. However, if we're going to harness the power of the team, these objectives should link into the team objectives and, in turn, the team objectives should connect into the organizational strategy.

```
        Organizational
           strategy

Individual          Team
objectives       objectives
```

Once a team has this true line of sight it should be easy for people to see where the organizational Results have been broken down into *what* the team is going to deliver and then where they as individual team members fit into that. Without this alignment, individual team members can feel like the work that they're doing is isolated and not making a difference to the mission of the team and organization.

In our experience, most teams are working on the right things, and they're working hard. They just fall into the trap of working on too much and diluting their focus or working on too many things that don't add the most value to the organization. They struggle to see the wood for the trees – to see the bigger picture beyond the task itself. They also struggle to prioritize what's the most important to free up their time and focus for the things that will make the biggest difference. This means that they feel overwhelmed, under-resourced and under-appreciated. It's hard for them to pace themselves and plan how best to pursue their goals. Creating clarity of accountabilities and then aligning them at all levels makes a huge difference to a team in terms of creating focus on the things that really matter and enabling a broader perspective.

Collaboration

When you don't have clarity of Results in a team, its members invariably end up working on their own tasks in a siloed manner. One of the things that leaders complain about to us the most is a lack of collaboration in their teams. Usually, the root cause of this is unclear Results. It's not that team members don't want to collaborate with others; they just don't know enough to do so well. Most team members want to collaborate with others, as they know that when they do they create better Relationships and outcomes (we look at Relationships in more depth in Chapter 5). They just don't have enough clarity to collaborate with each other. They're not truly clear on what everybody else is doing, how that links to their work and the value that they could add to other people, and vice versa. In some cases, this can lead to duplication of effort rather than collaboration, where team members are working on the same task without realizing it. Has that ever happened in your team?

Another benefit of clarity of Results is that it creates connections between team members. Just knowing what others in the team are working on creates a sense of solidarity, working together towards the Reason, even when the work itself is quite separate. It also offers an opportunity for people to support each other by offering ideas, best practices, suggestions and connections to other people outside the team. It breaks down the sense of isolation that people can feel when they're working on a task on their own, which is particularly important when a team is working remotely or in a hybrid way. It also creates more opportunities for inclusion and an appreciation of the skills and contributions of others in the team. This then creates more opportunities for real collaboration in the team.

> *'Ask your team to demonstrate what I call horizontal leadership – how can they be accountable for the results of the whole team including client impact, as well as their own results. This drives more enterprise thinking, stronger horizontal collaboration and healthy challenge amongst team members to deliver high performance.'*
>
> **Eric Schmidt**
> **Former CHRO, Pandora**

As a leader, it's essential that not only do you create clarity in your team about their accountabilities, but you also need to be clear when you want the team members involved to collaborate with others. Don't just leave it to chance. Facilitate the initiation of the collaboration and hold them accountable for collaborating with each other well.

Think about how you reward people for collaborating with others. This reinforces the expectation that they should collaborate to achieve better Results at both the individual and team level. How often do you ask your team members, 'Who have you collaborated with to achieve these Results?' or 'Who have you supported within the team to achieve Results?'

One leader we've worked with encourages his team members to collaborate and consult widely within the team as part of the problem-solving process before getting actively involved himself. This really drives a culture of mutual support in the team and a reduction in reliance on the leader to solve problems for them.

Over-collaboration

Some teams complain bitterly about a lack of time when we suggest that they should collaborate more effectively with each other. When this happens, it's often a signal that the team is 'over-collaborating'. What do we mean by this? This is when team members find themselves frequently in back-to-back meetings all day long, with no pause for breath. When they're reluctant to attend team meetings or they find themselves doing other things while at team meetings because they're not getting the value they need from those meetings. And it's not just meetings, it's other forms of collaboration too – instant messaging, email, text messages, phone calls, in fact any way in which team members communicate with each other. If these things aren't well managed by the team's Routines, the team will be in danger of over-collaborating and this will impact the Results of the team. In a team that's over-collaborating, things often get over-complicated, progress is slow and the team can repeatedly make poor decisions.

The organizational culture can affect the feeling of over-collaboration – what are the general expectations within the organization? Do people expect to be consulted, involved and included in everything? Do you find you need a meeting to plan a meeting and those meetings involve casts of thousands? Can team members easily manage these expectations or does going against that culture feel like pushing water uphill? In some cultures, it can feel like it goes against the grain to be really discerning about who needs to be involved in a task and who should really collaborate.

Over-collaboration can also be a sign of a lack of clarity and alignment in a team. Check back on your Results – are people clear about the team accountabilities and how their individual accountabilities align with them? Can you see where the most valuable opportunities are for collaboration and where there's really no need?

The 'Big Whats'

It's all very well saying that you need to create clarity for your team but how do you go about doing that? We've created a simple and effective way to get clarity on your Results, which has been used effectively with hundreds of teams. It's an interactive, collaborative process that enables the team to understand all the tasks that they're doing and then group them together into what we call the 'Big Whats'. This process articulates the team accountabilities in a simple, easy to remember way. This also means that every team member can see where their individual accountabilities sit within the 'Big Whats'. They can also see what everyone else is working on, their connection to the 'Big Whats', and the opportunities for collaboration in the team. As a leader, you'll get true clarity on what's going on in your team – often when we do this process, the leader gets some surprises!

Team case study
We worked with one team who were feeling particularly overwhelmed with their task list. They felt completely under-resourced and everything was urgent and important according to their stake-

holders. They said they didn't have time to collaborate with each other, let alone prioritize what was most important. We took them through the 'Big Whats' process and they identified four key accountabilities for the team.

Through the process, they were able to map everything to the 'Big Whats' and look at those four things through fresh eyes with a clear line of sight to their team Reason. They could also set out tangible measures for their 'Big Whats'. This in turn enabled them to reprioritize and change timelines for all their tasks. Their sense of overwhelm disappeared, they felt more in control and capable of achieving what was expected of them. When new requests came in from their stakeholders, they were able to review them against their 'Big Whats' and push back when needed to enable them to focus on the things they'd decided were the greatest value to the organization. When they couldn't say no to things, they were better equipped to have a conversation with their stakeholders about additional resources or reprioritizing their accountabilities, as the connections and impacts became so much clearer.

We encourage teams to articulate their 'Big Whats' and their connection to the Reason on one slide in the form of what we call a Diamond Team Charter.[13] The principle of

---

[13] See our website for a downloadable template: www.management-dynamics.com/leading-edge

having a way of visually representing the Reason and the Results for your team on one slide is a powerful tool to bring this to life.

The process

You can download a full description of the 'Big Whats' process from our website, but here's a quick overview of the process.

Make sure you have no more than five 'Big Whats' – you can have fewer, but not more. This is an exercise you can do on your own as leader for your team or, better still, together with your team.

- Brainstorm accountabilities:
    - Write down on sticky notes everything your team is accountable for. One sticky note per item. Keep going until you have everything.
- Cluster accountabilities:
    - Group the sticky notes together by theme – which ones naturally sit together? Try to put them into no more than five groups.
- Write an objective for each:
    - Each group should have at least one objective or KPI associated with it. For example, a 'Big What' of 'business growth' could have an objective of 'Revenue Growth of 30% by the end of the year.'
- Name the groups:
    - Name each group in such a way that it makes sense to others. Make sure they're BMI.
- Make the 'Big Whats' visible to you and the team:
    - Share the 'Big Whats' with your team and find a way to make them (and progress against them) visible

to everyone every day. For example, create a poster, put them on a whiteboard in the office, print them out and laminate them for everyone, put them on a team intranet site, etc. Whatever works for you and your team to keep them in line of sight.

Naming your 'Big Whats'

It's essential to give your 'Big Whats' BMI names. This is what helps the team to remember them, which is the key to them using them in their work. The purpose of this process is to give clarity about what they're working on and to help them prioritize and identify areas in which to collaborate. Make sure that they can do this, so remove any jargon, make them easy to understand, make sure that they resonate and recall what the essence of the accountability is to the team. Show them to people outside the team – if they don't understand straightaway, the name isn't right yet. You may need to keep coming back to this over time to refine it and find names that work. 'Big What' names work well when there's no jargon, they are short and sweet and they describe exactly what you'd expect each accountability to be about.

What if?

What happens if not everyone's accountabilities map to your 'Big Whats'? This occasionally happens in a team and it might highlight an issue with your team's organizational design. If one person's accountabilities are at complete odds with the rest of the team, you might need to ask yourself the hard question, 'Does this role actually belong in my team?' The answer might be that it doesn't but the role doesn't belong anywhere else either. Then you need to ask yourself how you can find some synergies between what they do and the rest of the team somewhere and somehow. Otherwise, that person will feel excluded from the team and you'll lose any potential benefits of what they can bring to the team, and vice versa.

The other thing to consider if this happens is whether you have identified the right 'Big Whats'. Is there another way of grouping the team's accountabilities that allows the excluded individual accountabilities to be included in one of the 'Big Whats'? Sometimes a simple reorganization of 'Big Whats' does the trick and creates a much more robust and compelling set of 'Big Whats' for the whole team.

Reviewing your 'Big Whats'

We're often asked how frequently a team should refresh and review their 'Big Whats'. There's no hard and fast rule for this and it's not necessarily something that has to be done every year as you would with your team members' individual objectives. The 'Big Whats' are generally more enduring than a 12-month process. They're quite fundamental to the team and, therefore, if you have got those 'Big Whats' right, you'll find that they last a long time. Having said that, it's good practice to have a Routine for reviewing them every now and again. Review the team's progress against the 'Big Whats', the various activities and tasks within them and where the collaboration lies. The real value comes from regular review into how your team is doing, what you could change, what the priorities are and how you're going to achieve those 'Big Whats'. Something that might trigger a review is changes in your team or in the organization. For example, if a restructure occurs and the expectations of your team have changed, usually this means that your 'Big Whats' need an update.

Aligning team members' accountabilities

Once you've identified your 'Big Whats', the process doesn't end there. The next step is to help your team members to align their accountabilities more tightly with the relevant 'Big Whats'. Do an exercise with your team to identify who in your team is contributing to which 'Big What'. It's important that each team member contributes to at least one, otherwise there may be an issue. Equally, don't expect everyone to be contributing to every 'Big What' in a significant way. This can just lead to over-collaboration within your team, where everybody is involved in everything, which can lead to confusion and overload. Doing an alignment exercise is a great opportunity for individuals to look at the 'Big Whats' and reconsider their task list, removing any duplication or low-value and redundant tasks.

Once you've created alignment of accountabilities in your team, the next stage is to encourage collaboration on the things that matter the most. You're not looking for collaboration for collaboration's sake – this just creates more work for everybody and feels like collaboration is being done without a purpose. What you're looking for is collaboration with meaning. If you use the 'Big Whats' as the basis for collaboration efforts, then people are collaborating with a purpose and on the right things – the things that really matter to your team.

When we were first testing out this process, we encouraged our team to collaborate more without much focus on what they collaborated on. One month later we were shocked, looking at how they were spending their time, that they were collaborating on absolutely everything. They were complaining about even more overload and we learned how important it is to ensure that collaboration is done well and with purpose. It's important to be careful about how you set the scene for collaboration and that it's set within the context of those 'Big Whats' and what they're really trying to achieve from a Results perspective.

The links to other Edge Dynamics

Results are crucial in a high-performing team and create clarity for your team on what they're accountable for delivering. They also create the foundation for success in all the other Edge Dynamics.

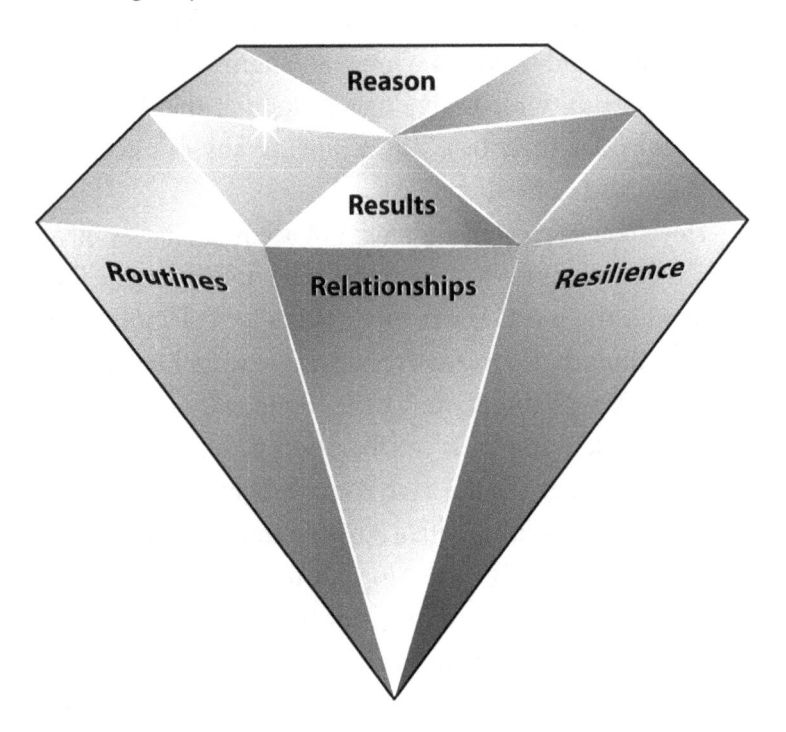

The connection to Reason

When we were discussing Reason in Chapter 2, we talked about how teams can get confused between Reason and Results (the *why* and the *what*). It's essential when talking about Results that they're connected to the Reason. *What* the team is accountable for doing has to be based on *why* you're doing it in the first place. Being able to articulate how the team's Results support the pursuit of the team Reason is essential for any team.

When a team works on tasks in isolation of the Reason, they risk the work feeling relentless and without purpose. Remember, it's the *why* that taps into your team's intrinsic motivation, which lights up how they feel about the work that they're doing.

Resignations are driven mostly by a lack of connection to their *why* at work. People often leave jobs because they've lost sight of the Reason in that role and have decided to seek fulfilment of purpose elsewhere. The *what* is just not enough on its own.

The connection to Relationships

When you have clear and aligned Results you create space for better Relationships in your team. When you have clarity and alignment in your team, it's possible for your team members to collaborate well because they have a visible reason for doing so. They're more likely to communicate well with others because they have a shared common goal. They're also likely to build trust with others because they want to prove themselves to be reliable at delivering what they say they're going to deliver. They know what people are working on and have a shared accountability, so they want to support their colleagues, and vice versa.

The connection to Routines

Clarity of Results is crucial in enabling a team to design their team's Routines well. When you have clear, aligned team accountabilities you can be sure that the right Routines will be easy to identify and implement.

When a team has created clear team accountabilities, they have a desire to have visibility of their Results, and to track their progress. This is enabled by the team's Routines and helps them to not only focus on the value-added stuff, but also see the bigger picture.

The connection to Resilience

When a team isn't clear on its Results, it's difficult to have high levels of Resilience (see Chapter 6). Clarity is essential to managing your team members' workloads, and without it they'll likely feel overwhelmed and exhausted. When you clarify accountabilities in your team, you're giving them two gifts at once:

- First, you're giving them the gift of focus – focus on what adds the greatest value to the organization.
- Second, you're giving them the gift of seeing the big picture, as well as line of sight to the organizational goals and the team Reason.

These two gifts at first glance might seem like they're contradictory – can you focus while also seeing the bigger picture? We would argue that a high-performing team needs to be able to do both at the same time and that both are crucial to the Resilience of the team. We would also argue that it's impossible to do either without clear and aligned Results. When we've worked with teams on their Results, we've seen very clear improvements in the teams' Resilience.

A high-performing team consistently achieves its KPIs, regardless of the challenges that pop up. They have the Resilience to keep going, even when the going gets tough. They can reprioritize their Results as needed and maintain focus on the things that are absolutely essential to the success of the team.

> ### Results – a summary
> Results are *what* the team is accountable for delivering. They're measured through team KPIs/goals/objectives.
>
> One of the biggest gifts that you can give your team is clarity, and clarity of Results is essential for a high-performing team. Teams with the greatest lack of clarity around Results are often competing and maybe even undermining the work of others in the team. A lack of clarity is a key root cause of overload and overwhelm in a team.
>
> Team Results are multilayered and there needs to be alignment at all levels: individual objectives should link into the team objectives and, in turn, the team objectives should connect into the organizational strategy.
>
> Clarity of Results creates connections between team members and enables collaboration, which creates opportunities for team members to offer each other ideas, best

practice and suggestions. This is also the foundation for complex problem-solving.

Over-collaboration can also be a sign of a lack of clarity and alignment in a team. Check back on your Results – are people clear about the team accountabilities and how their individual accountabilities align with them?

Use the 'Big Whats' process to create clarity of the team's accountabilities in a simple, easy to remember format.

Results impact all the other Edge Dynamics positively and pave the way for a high-performing team.

CHAPTER 4

Routines

Ensure that all your Routines (meetings, ways of working, etc.) drive all the other Edge Dynamics and support high performance rather than interfere with it. Know how to make decisions in your team.

Defining Routines

Routines are a team's ways of working. The rhythms, tools and processes they use to get things done. This includes how they keep each other informed and up to date on the various tasks, projects and information they need to deliver their Results well. It's also about how they make decisions and who needs to be involved in the process. It includes reviews of workloads and changes that are coming up that might affect the team and where adjustments might need to be made. Routines enable the Edge Dynamics in your team to work. They need to be designed well to do this, otherwise they will have the opposite effect.

Routines dictate the pace of a team and, if you're not careful, they can get in the way of the effectiveness of the team and slow it down. Routines can sometimes be heavy, burdensome, administrative or even bureaucratic and out of date. Routines should allow the team to work at a pace that really suits them and the work that they're doing. At their worst, Routines will destroy Relationships (Chapter 5), undermine your Results (Chapter 3), obscure your Reason (Chapter 2) and destroy the team's Resilience (Chapter 6). They may contribute to burnout and absence in your team, so make sure that you design them well. How often do you hear people in the team saying, 'Oh no, not another meeting!' or 'That meeting was a waste of time,' or 'I have to complete another spreadsheet for some reason and I don't see how it adds value.' These comments are symptoms of ineffective or poor Routines.

Routines, like much in your team, need to be dynamic and ever-changing. Constantly review your Routines to ensure that they remain fit for purpose and that they're driving all the other Edge Dynamics. Across the hundreds of teams that we've worked with, we see out-of-date Routines. This is often because a team has inherited old Routines or has just got complacent about how things are 'done around here'. Routines can easily get stuck or become obsolete when the team hasn't reviewed their Routines for effectiveness. In the first Advantycs® diagnostic, Routines are often the thing mentioned the most in the stop/start/continue comments from the team, and they're almost always easy quick wins to change.

Look out for the signs that your team Routines no longer work. For example, has attendance at your team meetings dropped? Are people no longer following a process in the team? Are people using different methods to communicate with each other than you had previously agreed? Teams can easily change and adjust their Routines, and the benefits are quickly felt. Regularly ask your team for feedback on Routines. This will ensure that you're continuously improving them and adapting them to the changing needs of your team.

Creating a team rhythm

When you're crafting your Routines, start by thinking about what rhythm your team needs to have to deliver on its Results, develop and maintain good Relationships and ensure high levels of Resilience. Your team's rhythm needs to work with the team, not against the team. What's the right cadence of meetings, communications and interaction that reinforces good Relationships and enables the delivery of Results? What cadence connects the team to their team Reason? What will enable a good balance of meetings versus time to actually do the work without creating overwhelm and over-collaboration? Getting team members together to discuss operational aspects is important. However, it's also important to discuss how the team is making progress against their Reason, what Relationships are like in the team and whether there are more opportunities for collaboration. How can they have more discussion and greater levels of challenge in the team? When do people have development conversations, both individually but also as a team?

Crafting the Routines for your team is an art, not a science. It needs to be ever-changing to meet the dynamic needs of the team. Personality will play a big part in how you craft the rhythm of your team Routines. For example, the introverts in your team will need time to reflect and prepare for meetings and may find spending all their time in meetings frustrating and demotivating to the point of burnout. Likewise, the extroverts will need time to discuss and think out loud to come up with new ideas and move their work forward. Striking a balance for both needs is essential. You'll also need to consider the experience levels within your team. Less experienced people might need more contact time and more support in terms of connecting with others. This enables them to learn, bounce ideas off more experienced people and build their confidence. Others might be more able to steam ahead without those interactions. Considering how you can develop them as mentors for other members of the team can strengthen Relationships.

It's very easy to over-engineer the Routines for your team. Less is definitely more. Keep reviewing your Routines to see how you can remove or shorten meetings, not add new ones in. Continuously review how the team communicates with each other to make it simpler and easier for them to do so. Regularly look at processes to see how they can be streamlined or removed. Consider the tools the team uses for all of this. Are they fit for purpose still? Are there other tools out there that would make things easier for the team? Could the way that the team use tools be adjusted so that they become more flexible and more fit for purpose?

Meetings

Teams that we work with consistently complain about meetings, and research shows that the number of meetings people spend their time in has increased dramatically over the last few years. According to the 2021 Productivity Trends Report, professionals are attending nearly 26 meetings a week, which equates to just over five meetings per day. That number has increased massively since COVID-19 started, by a staggering 70% since February 2020.[14] Working virtually creates more meetings. The average meeting time was found to be 50

---

[14] Reclaimai 2021 Productivity Trends Report: https://reclaim.ai/blog/productivity-report-one-on-one-meetings

minutes, which means that people are spending over half of their week just in meetings. No wonder team members are complaining about overload!

When creating your rhythm for team meetings, consider who needs to attend. What's the desired outcome of this meeting for the team? What does the agenda need to be for maximum effectiveness? How will you communicate that agenda so that the introverts have time to reflect and prepare for the meeting? How will you structure the agenda so that the extroverts have the chance to think out loud and brainstorm ideas? How will you ensure that the actions are taken and that progress is made as a result of the meeting? How does the meeting add value to the whole team, not just key individuals within it? Does inviting everybody to the meeting create inclusion or does it just result in frustration for some who might feel they're wasting their time? Challenge your own and your team's thinking about whether the meeting is needed in the first place. Is there another way to achieve the outcome? There are effective, interactive online tools where teams can share ideas without everyone being in the same place at the same time. Get your team members to research options and find ones they'd like to try using.

When considering who should participate in a meeting, think about who will be able to contribute to the outcome. This might mean setting up smaller groups for certain key meetings. It's important to be able to articulate to the rest of the team why they're not included in those meetings and for them to not feel excluded. Help them to understand that it's much more about effective use of time. It's also important to know when to include the wider team in these smaller groups to improve outcomes through brainstorming, challenge and playing devil's advocate. This can strengthen connection to the team Reason and Relationships.

Also, consider the Routines you have in your team for 1-2-1s. How do you keep track of and engage with each team member within your team? For example, you might have a rhythm of 1-2-1 catch-ups with your team members. Some leaders like to do this weekly, some fortnightly, some monthly – the frequency depends on you and how often you need to connect with different team members and they with you. It might also vary from team member to team member, depending on their capability and their experience. Alongside these general catch-up meetings, which are about tracking individual progress against team objectives, it's important to also catch up regularly with your team members on their development. We would recommend a minimum of quarterly meetings with each person to discuss development plans, aspirations and progress. When you have a 1-2-1 rhythm, your team meetings transform into so much more. They'll be about discussing the team's shared goals and opportunities. This is so much more effective than sitting round the table or virtual room listening to everybody's individual operational update, which, let's face it, can be really boring! Keep your team meetings engaging and inspirational and a space where everybody can feel included and not wishing they were somewhere else, getting on with their own work.

Decision-making: who makes decisions in your team?

A key Routine in any team is how decisions are made. Your team has to be clear on the process for making decisions and this must include who actually makes the decision. Is it you as the leader or are your team empowered to make some decisions for themselves? If you're not clear about this, either all the decisions will be made by you, or the team will make inappropriate decisions at the wrong level. If you're making all the decisions yourself, there's a danger you'll become a bottleneck for the team and they'll be waiting for your decision before they can progress on things. This can slow work down. From research, we know that a team makes better decisions than one person alone.[15] This is because teams will debate and brainstorm options more effectively than one person will on their own. It's also because many decisions require complex thinking, which is harder to do alone.

If you're holding on to too many decisions yourself, you might find yourself unable to take a vacation without your team members getting in touch with you. You might find that your availability to make a decision dictates the speed at which that decision can be made. Ask yourself whether you really need to make that decision. This is important to ensure that decisions are being made at the right level. Then consider the impact that changing circumstances can have. It's appropriate for you to say, 'Most of the time, when things are normal, I don't need to be involved. However, if the situation changes or there's a crisis, I need to be informed or I need to be involved.' Often, leaders hold on to decision-making because of the fear of a potential crisis, regardless of whether there really is a crisis. This disempowers your team and places

---

[15] www.forbes.com/sites/eriklarson/2017/09/21/new-research-diversity-inclusion-better-decision-making-at-work/?sh=68bcdc674cbf

an over-reliance on you. Consider whether this is just a way of stroking your own ego.

One way to assess whether decisions are being made at the right level within your team is to track for a few weeks how many decisions are escalated to you as leader, or how many decisions you just make by yourself. If most of the decisions are being made by you, this could be an indication of a lack of empowerment in your team. Review the list of decisions that you have made and consider which ones could be made by your team members without you. Also, have a look at the types of decisions that are being made. Are you making decisions about the most appropriate things? Are you adding value to the decisions that are made? How can you lift the capability of your team to take on more of these decisions? Discuss this with your team and come up with some criteria as to when it would be appropriate to involve you or not.

We discuss the processes that you can use for gaining agreement to decisions that are made in the team under Relationships (Chapter 5). We look at how to get commitment from the team to the decisions once they've been made in that chapter. It's also important to have a Routine for documenting the decisions that are made by the team, to keep track of those decisions and their associated actions. How will you document, record and track progress of decisions that you make? Some teams that we work with use a decision-tracker spreadsheet that lists all the decisions that they've made as a team and associated actions, along with who's accountable for making sure those actions are followed up.

Communication

There are lots of ways in which teams communicate with each other. The most obvious one is email, and many teams use instant messaging services, collaboration tools and virtual meeting software.

Email

Let's start by looking at email as a form of communication between team members. Research shows that the average office worker will receive 121 emails per day and sends 40 emails per day. And yet the average opening rate is only 20% to 40%.[16] That's a lot of unnecessary emails. We would suggest that a lot of email traffic is generated by your own team, so it's important to consider carefully how email is used within your team. Be deliberate yourself and get your team to think about who they want to include in emails.

When you're writing an email, challenge yourself in the use of CC. People often use CC to keep people informed or cover their own backs. The sender thinks that they're CCing someone just to keep them informed, while the receiver assumes that they might need to do something with that email. They spend time reading the email with an action in mind only to find out at the end of the email that no action was required. This creates duplication of effort, wastes people's time and erodes Relationships. The other problem with CC is that, once it starts being used in an email, the

---

[16] Source: Radicati: www.radicati.com/wp/wp-content/uploads/2017/12/Email-Statistics-Report-2018-2022-Executive-Summary.pdf

follow-up emails replying to this email also CC everyone. It can be really hard to track actions for those in CC.

We would propose a better methodology to keep people informed and up to date with progress is to never use the CC box. Only email people who really need to take action as a result of reading your message. In this way, they know that they need to do something with the email. Use the @ function in popular email applications to help with this. If you want someone to take action, you can embed the person's email address in your email and it will automatically send the email to them with their name highlighted next to the action.

Also, consider the power of the subject header in your emails. One leader we worked with agreed with his team to use the subject header to identify when/who action was required by and a deadline date. This way team members know whether they're meant to take action and by when before opening the email.

These are just some suggestions. The most important thing is to talk about your use of email as a team and how you can make it an effective tool. Discuss how you can eliminate the barriers your team has in place so that email becomes an enabling Routine rather than a disabling one.

Ensure that email is being used appropriately in your team. For example, should team members email each other just for quick questions? Is there a more appropriate way of asking those same questions? Could they send each other an instant message instead or pick up the phone and call each other? This implies that the question is urgent and needs an immediate response. In this example, email could just be used for the less urgent enquiries.

There's no one standard way of using email across teams. The most important thing is to agree with your team how to use it effectively and intentionally.

Instant messaging

Instant messaging can be an effective tool for communicating quickly with team members both professionally and socially. While we were writing this book, our team members were sharing photos on WhatsApp of a large event going on with a big client of ours. It was lovely to be able to feel part of that in some small way and to share their excitement about the event. We could also ask some questions and they could respond really quickly.

It's a tool that feels light and low on bureaucracy, and it's informal. However, it's important to set some expectations around the use of tools such as instant messaging. Their 'always on' nature can mean that team members feel a responsibility to respond to messages at all hours. Make sure the team is taking care to not overuse these tools outside of working hours. Often these tools can be available on team members' personal mobile phones and devices, so it's also important to agree ground rules around appropriate content and maintain the standards of behaviour that you've agreed through your work on Relationships (see Chapter 6).

Collaboration tools

There are many very good collaboration tools on the market that can help teams to work together on projects and keep everything in one place. They can track tasks and share thoughts and ideas with each other easily. It's important to have one way of collaborating through technology across the team. Agree with your team which tool is the most appropriate for the needs of the team and stick with that. We see lots of teams with a myriad of different tools. These tools can creep in over time, maybe because a new team member likes a particular tool, and before you know it a team has four different collaboration tools on the go at once, which can be overwhelming and confusing. Be deliberate about which tool you'll use as a team, when and why. Make sure everybody understands when you use the tool and that they all commit to using the tool. Agree to regularly review your collaboration tools, as technology and needs are always changing. The available tools regularly change, so challenge your team to keep abreast of what's on the market and what will improve the effectiveness of the team.

Processes

Another example of a Routine that you'll no doubt have in your team is processes. These are standardized ways in which things get done in your team. No matter what kind of team you have, you'll have a process of some kind for various things. These may or may not have been documented and they'll vary in complexity from one team to another. However, it's important to be aware of what they are. The more you can streamline and simplify your team's processes the better. Likewise, the more you can document key processes in your team, the more likely your team members are to follow them consistently without having to start from scratch each time. The key here is to keep it simple and appropriate for the type of work your team is doing. We have a team of project consultants and we like to create consistency about how they work with our clients. That doesn't mean we need a massive, detailed manual of everything that they do in their roles. A quick video demonstrating how to do certain tasks is all that's required. When new people join the team, this makes it easy to induct them into their role, and we review these processes regularly.

While reviewing and challenging processes, consider their purpose. In some organizations we've seen individuals, teams and indeed the organization as a whole use processes to avoid risk, individual accountability, innovation and restrict change and adaptation. Sometimes processes have been used to avoid direct interactions and discussions. Sometimes they've been designed to avoid the 1% case of corruption rather than the 99% cases of delivering efficiently. 'I followed the process,' is a get out of jail free card for any other poor behaviour or performance. Teams need to review processes and make them fit for purpose. Anti-corruption and compliance activities can be covered, while ensuring that processes are fit for purpose and adapted to the changing context of the team and individuals.

Escalations

Escalations are when things go wrong in a team and the team brings something to your attention as leader. They're also when a team member asks for help at a higher level. Escalations are important in a team and they can be a symptom of other things going on in the team at a deeper level. As leader, you can track escalations to you by the team over a period of time – say a couple of weeks. Look back and notice what kinds of things are being escalated to you and what might be driving those escalations. Are there particular individuals who escalate more than other individuals? Does one individual escalate things to you that they're unsure about, suggesting that they might have an issue with confidence?

There are four main reasons why team members escalate things to their leader:

- Capability – they don't have the capability to complete the task
- Confidence – they don't have confidence to solve the problem
- Knowledge – they don't have enough knowledge to inform a decision or solve a problem
- Authority – they don't perceive that they have the authority to make the decision or solve the problem

Capability Do they have the capability to complete the task?	**Confidence** Do they have the confidence to solve the problem?
Knowledge Do they have enough knowledge to inform a decision or solve a problem?	**Authority** Do they perceive that they have the authority to make the decision or solve the problem?

Once you've identified the most frequent causes of escalations in your team, you can take action to fill the gaps that you've identified. For example, if a lot of the escalations are due to *capability* gaps, you could organize some training around that particular topic. If it's about *confidence*, talk to them about what they need to gain more courage in and reassure them of their skills and experience. Encourage them to have a go and give them permission to fail if it's appropriate. If they don't have the *knowledge* to inform a decision or solve a problem, coach them on where they could get that knowledge, without just giving them the answer. If they perceive that they don't have the *authority* to make a decision or solve a problem, challenge yourself and them as to how you can provide them with that authority.

Planning and adjusting work

Workload is the number-one issue we hear about in every team. There's always more work than any team can ever complete. Learning to review, prioritize, reallocate and adjust work is a critical skill for teams. One of the benefits of a high-performing team is using the whole team as a pool of resource for work. The whole team should feel accountable for the team's Results and should regularly review how they're doing and where work needs to be adjusted. New work will come in and priorities might have to shift. What Routines do you need to have in place so that the team are a part of this review process? How can you ensure that they feel that they can contribute by offering more resource to other team members?

Engaging externally (e.g. customers, suppliers, partners)

Teams don't operate in isolation. They're part of a system of customers, stakeholders and other teams inside and outside the organization. It's therefore important to consider how the team engages with each of these groups and how they manage

Relationships more effectively. To build strong Relationships with all these different parties, the team needs to think about what regular Routines are in place and what communications and information processes need to be established. Review what the team currently has in place, then identify what works and what needs to be changed.

Accountability

In a good team we see leaders effectively holding their team accountable for both the Results and Relationships in the team. In a high-performing team, we see team members taking on this role themselves alongside the leader. They hold each other mutually accountable for doing what they say they're going to do. What does this look like? In a good team, if somebody doesn't deliver on something that they said they were going to, other team members may go to the leader and tell them. The expectation is that the leader will resolve it for them. In a high-performing team, team members will go directly to the person who has under-delivered and talk to them directly about it. They'll do so in a manner of constructive challenge without it descending into destructive conflict. They'll try to support and understand the other team member in what's preventing them from meeting their commitments. This is a fundamental difference between a good and a high-performing team – one that makes an enormous impact on both you as leader and the Relationships in the team. Having Routines that enable accountability in your team is important. As is thinking about your behaviour as a leader in the team and your expectations of accountability.

'What you say in a meeting room is what you do outside the meeting room.'

**Frederic Debrosses
General Manager, Middle East, Africa,
Global Business Development, JDE Peet's**

In a high-performing team, you may not realize explicitly that accountability is taking place within the team. You may only notice the absence of escalations to you as leader by team members. It may become visible through some of the lessons learned that team members might share in team meetings, proposals they make to update a process or discussions about sharing workload in a different way. They may request some training to upskill certain team members in broader skills. These are just some of the indications that the team members are proactively being accountable for how they can get the work done together without involving you. When this happens, it's revolutionary as a leader. You'll feel lighter, like you no longer have the full weight of responsibility for everything in the team on your shoulders alone. You'll be consistently impressed with what your team is capable of.

Let's look at some examples of how you can craft your Routines so that they reinforce this kind of accountability in your team.

Share the role of chair

First of all, reflect on how you run team meetings. Do you always chair the meeting, or could you share that role around your team? By taking on the role of chair, team members are practising holding each other accountable for things such as team Results. All of these ideas promote the development of the skill of accountability in the team.

Ensure that your team work together

When team members escalate issues to you instead of solving the problem, you can say that you'll only talk to them once they've spoken to other members of the team first. This means that you ensure that they work together to try to solve a problem or at least come up with some options for solutions before coming to you.

> *'The value creation from your team is a function of the time you're prepared to invest in their coaching and support.'*
>
> **Neil Molyneux**
> **Technical Innovation Group Director, PepsiCo**

Encourage direct communication

When team members come to you talking about issues with other team members, ask them whether they've spoken to that team member first before coming to you. Only engage in that conversation once they've spoken to them.

As leaders, we can sometimes rob our team members of accountability inadvertently. This can happen when we micromanage people in the team and engage in activities that are operational and at too low a level of detail for the role that we have in the team. If this is a tendency for you, consider how you can step out of the detail and into bigger picture thinking, while ensuring that the details are taken care of by the team. An excuse we hear from leaders is that the team's workload is so great that they have to step in to do some of this operational work. As a leader, you'll never have time and space to think more strategically and take on that bigger picture if you're down in the weeds working with your team regularly. Re-evaluate what you're spending your time and focus on to enable you to move up and out of the operational into becoming more strategic.

Another thing that might rob your team of accountability is a belief that you as a leader need to understand everybody's roles and jobs and what they do to manage them well. This is a limiting belief as it means that you'll only be able to lead a team of a certain size and scope before this burns you out. It can also cause a tendency to meddle and do things yourself rather than ensuring that your team members do it themselves. The best thing you can do is to take the opportunity to manage people with limited knowledge and experience of the details of their job. Actively seek to stay out of the detail. This is what general management is all about and is a core skill of all senior leaders. If you don't master this, not only are you creating a lack of accountability in your team, but you're also blocking your own future as you won't be able to progress to bigger and broader roles.

The links to the other Edge Dynamics

Routines are key to how the team operates together. When the Routines are fit for purpose, it creates a foundation for the other Edge Dynamics to be optimally successful.

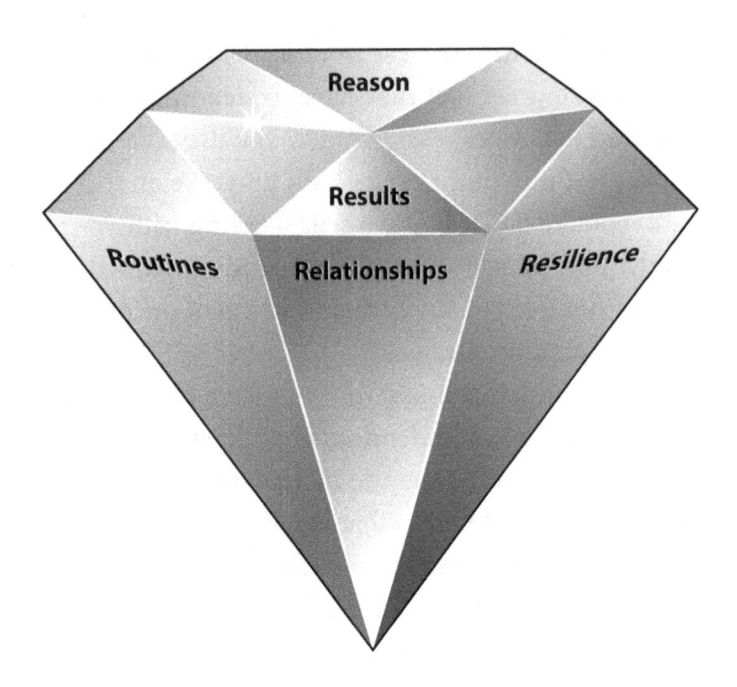

The connection to Reason

A high-performing team has a Routine for reviewing and refreshing their team Reason regularly. They also have a Routine for reconnecting with their team Reason, even if they don't change it. They regularly discuss the Reason and bring it into their everyday operation.

The connection to Results

A high-performing team recognizes that Results require regular focus, tracking and review. This means that Routines for Results are essential. Without them, a team never really knows where they are in relation to their Results. Are they performing or not? If they don't adjust their Routines, their Routines may no longer enable the delivery of Results and may, in fact, get in the way.

The connection to Relationships

Poor Routines can be very damaging to Relationships in a team. When Routines are ineffective, they can create frustration and conflict and undermine collaboration in a team. Effective Routines support the development of Relationships in a team by encouraging collaboration and communication among team members.

The connection to Resilience

Ineffective Routines can wear people down by wasting their time and sapping them of energy. Meetings are a great example of this – long meetings with a lack of focus and outcome truly frustrate people and exhaust them. The ineffective use of tools such as email can also create huge workloads that add little value and drain team members of energy. Effective Routines have the opposite effect and help people to manage their energy levels and workloads effectively, while also providing the opportunity for people to support each other in the team.

Routines – a summary

Routines are a team's ways of working and they interact with Relationships and Resilience to support *how* the team operates. Routines enable all the Edge Dynamics in your team to work. They need to be designed well.

Routines, like much in your team, need to be dynamic and ever-changing. Constantly review your Routines to ensure that they remain fit for purpose and that they're driving all the other Edge Dynamics. They need to be ever-changing to meet the dynamic needs of the team.

Start to design your team's Routines by thinking about what rhythm your team needs to deliver on its Results, develop and maintain good Relationships and ensure high levels of Resilience.

Design your team meeting cadence carefully and consider the frequency, attendees and agenda.

Be clear about who makes decisions on what in your team. A team makes better decisions than one person alone, so how can you ensure that your team is involved appropriately in decisions and that you don't make all the decisions yourself as leader?

Help your team to communicate effectively with each other via email, instant messaging and collaboration tools. Design Routines about the use of these communication channels and help the team to adhere to them. Ensure that your team processes are documented sufficiently without being cumbersome to maintain. Track the things your team members are escalating to you and work to understand the root causes so that over time you can minimize them.

In a high-performing team, the members hold each other mutually accountable for doing what they say they're going to do. Create accountability in your team by sharing the role of the meeting chair, getting your team to work together on projects and encouraging direct communication between team members.

CHAPTER 5

Relationships

Build the appropriate levels of trust in the team. Ensure that diverse opinions and points of view are embraced. Help the team disagree well and overcome conflict.

Definition of Relationships

Relationships are the cornerstone of a high-performing team and, if you want your team to reach their potential, you need to invest in creating high-quality Relationships. Without effective Relationships, a team is not a team – they're just a bunch of people who all happen to work for the same boss. Relationships are, in essence, the interactions between the individuals in a team and how much value those interactions bring to the team and the achievement of their Results and Reason.

> *'Some teams just don't work and you need to understand why fast.'*
>
> **Neil Molyneux**
> **Technical Innovation Group Director, PepsiCo**

Having great Relationships doesn't mean to say team members have to be best friends with everybody in the team, but what they do need is to have mutual respect, an understanding of each other and a way to communicate and collaborate that's truly effective. The team also needs to feel free to share their opinions and to have their opinions listened to.

The benefits of great Relationships

Relationships help your team make great quality decisions. Team members make better decisions when Relationships are good because it means they get challenge, discussion and ultimately greater buy-in from their colleagues. When teams have better Relationships, they also have more fun and enjoyment from the work they're doing. Human beings are social animals, which means that they like to feel connected to others and they enjoy the community that comes with a sense of team. Some of the most fun we've ever had at work has been in teams where we've got on with most people. Sometimes the work is really tough, but it's that sense of belonging and support that really made the difference to us, even in difficult times. If there's one Edge Dynamic that at the end of the day really makes the difference to a high-performing team, it's the Relationships.

When have you felt like you've been part of a high-performing team? What were the Relationships like in that team? We bet that they were pretty good, that you could say what you wanted to say (constructively) without fear of offending others, that you could share how you felt about things, that others held you accountable and challenged you on your thinking to help you to make decisions. This is Relationships at their best.

Relationships are the foundation of a high-performing team, and investing in building Relationships is essential if you want your team to get beyond mediocre to high performance. Most people resonate with this in some way at an intuitive level. However, Relationships will also be the downfall of a team, as no team can remain high-performing for long if Relationships aren't great. This is the key to sustaining high performance over a long period of time.

In the absence of all the other Edge Dynamics, good Relationships enable a team to deal with change, volatility and ambiguity for short periods of time. They're the glue that can hold a team together for a while. Teams are dynamic, so if the Relationships are good this means that the team members have the flexibility to support each other as they shift their focus.

However, this won't sustain a team for very long and our experience shows that all the Edge Dynamics are essential for maintaining long-term high performance.

At the same time, without good Relationships, no matter how strong all the other Edge Dynamics are, the team will start to get frustrated with each other and the sense of community will disintegrate. No team can withstand this for long.

The complexity of Relationships

Relationships are also the most complex of all the Edge Dynamics. Teams are made up of people, and people are complex beings. They're all different, they all have different needs. Relationships are also not static, they're always changing. A team is made up of different personalities and these change over time. People come and go within the team and, every time a new person joins the team, the team changes. Every time somebody leaves the team, the team changes. This means that Relationships are incredibly dynamic and constantly need investment and effort to maintain them over time.

Teams are an organic system. The system consists of key players and interactions that are all interconnected. Many of those connections are explicit and we can see what they are, but many of them are implicit and are harder to identify. For example, you can explicitly see who gets on well within a team. They might meet each other for a virtual coffee or a social night out or just choose to work together regularly. Implicitly, it might be harder to identify where there are sources of tension or what really motivates a particular individual in a team. Team dynamics are more complex than we can ever imagine and sometimes we can be surprised by certain things that happen in teams. As an organic system, teams continually evolve as people come and go and this impacts the team. As a leader, therefore, you need to consistently observe the Relationships in the team. You need to consider how you and the team are affecting all the different variables within your team.

Teams also don't work in isolation. They're part of a broader context. A broader system of the other teams in the organization, suppliers and customers, all of whom have impacts on the Relationships within the team. Getting your team to consider that wider context and the key Relationships that they have, not only within the team but also external to the team, is crucial to getting to and sustaining high performance in a team.

You also need to consider the systems that people are part of outside of work. People aren't just 'work beings', they have a whole personal, human life outside of work. They bring this with them to work every day and this can also have an impact on the team system. You'll notice when one of your team members comes in to work in a bad mood and that can influence everybody on the team in some way. What happened to them to cause that? Having compassion for that is critical within a team, without being intrusive.

Where do you start with Relationships?

So where do you start when developing your team's Relationships? We've identified several key skills that teams need to develop to be truly high-performing when it comes to their Relationships. They're divided into two levels: the foundation skills that team members need to have good solid Relationships, and what we call the stretch skills that will truly take your team to the next level. Your team won't achieve the stretch skills until you've developed the foundation skills.

Foundation Relationship skills	Stretch Relationship skills
Team members understand each other and have mutual respect	Team members have vulnerability-based trust
Team members are clear about what expected behaviours are in the team	Team members are willing to admit mistakes
Team members strive consistently to demonstrate expected behaviours in the team	Team members ask each other for help

Team members demonstrate reliability-based trust	Team members constructively challenge each other in the service of better outcomes
Team members commit to decisions made by the team	Team members proactively include others

Foundation skills

These are the skills that team members need to have good solid Relationships.

Team members understand each other and have mutual respect

To have a good foundation of Relationships in a team, its members need to know each other well enough to understand each other's personality traits, what motivates them and what drives their behaviour on a day-to-day basis. When team members don't understand each other very well this can lead to misunderstandings and assumptions being made about what's driving that person's behaviour. It's particularly important when you have a very diverse group of people in your team to understand that people have different ways of looking at the world, different values and different ways of thinking. Investing in understanding each other better can really ease some of those misunderstandings. It also challenges people to think about the view they have of what can be 'right' and to see that there can be many ways and many approaches to things. It helps people to realize that there's no one or right way to do or see things. This is the route to better decision-making in teams.

There are several different personality tools available, all with their strengths and limitations. Our advice would be to pick a tool that works for your team. Does it resonate with them and their context? Is it easy for them to remember and therefore use? Can it help them discuss how they communicate and behave with each other? Does it promote curiosity about how other people see the world? Does it challenge stereotypes rather than providing excuses for certain behaviours? Does it encourage people to start to flex how they behave with others who might have a different preference to them?

Mutual respect comes from knowing each other better. This is team members understanding each other's strengths within the team. It's knowing a bit more about who they are as a human being and what they stand for. It's about understanding their personal values and what's important to them in work and life, their individual *why* (See Chapter 2). It's about knowing a bit about the experiences that they've gone through and some of the challenges and achievements that they've had. Investing time in helping team members to share and learn about all of this will enrich and create the foundation of good Relationships in your team. Also, when new people join it's important that there's some way of inducting them into this process.

All of this creates a sense of curiosity about people in the team who may be different to other team members. Difference is an interesting thing when it comes to human beings. We actively push against difference and look for similarity in others – it's very natural and is an unconscious, deep-rooted safety mechanism. However, in a team, difference can be incredibly valuable. It helps us to think differently about things and to solve problems in innovative ways. It helps us to make better decisions based on a broader perspective.

Through difference, we face complexity with more ease. Embracing difference and helping people to move past their own desire for sameness is essential in a high-performing team.

With all of this, a one-off 'team-building event' will never be enough. You'll need to invest more time and effort than this and find ways to incorporate it into your day-to-day interactions with each other, otherwise it will remain an intellectual exercise and not have the impact that you need.

> **Team case study**
>
> We worked with a project team recently who were experiencing a real disconnect in their Relationships. There were a lot of 'elephants in the room' – things that were there but not mentioned. Conflict was a constant undercurrent and people were frustrated and fatigued by the lack of cohesion. There was almost no trust in this team. In fact, could you really call them a team at all? If it wasn't for the fact that they all worked for the same boss and apparently had the same goal, we would have been questioning this.
>
> It was obvious that the first place to start with this team was on Relationships. We helped them to understand that the source of their lack of cohesion was their core misunderstanding of each other and the root cause of their behaviour. We worked with a personality tool that gave them a simple framework for understanding the motives of themselves and others. Almost immediately they recognized

> what was driving their differences and therefore what the source of their conflict and disconnect was. There were several 'aha' moments in that first session together. They were able to establish new ways of connecting with each other on a basis of mutual respect and they started to discuss ways to disagree well with each other without it descending into open conflict. They now use the language they learned to communicate much more effectively with each other and to resolve misunderstandings immediately.

Team members are clear about expected behaviours in the team

Another skill that's crucial for creating the foundation of good Relationships in your team is for team members to be clear about the behaviours that are expected of them. All team members have expectations of behaviours. The trouble is they might have different expectations from each other! Very few teams put the effort into clearly articulating and agreeing between them what they'd like those behaviours to be. Behaviours generally evolve over time and may or may not be constructive and helpful for the Relationships in the team. It's important to invest time as a team in carefully crafting the behaviours that you'd like to see demonstrated.

It's not hard to have a conversation with your team about the behaviours that they expect to see demonstrated in the team. You can facilitate a short meeting to brainstorm and prioritize what those behaviours should be. Once you've agreed them, it's important to make sure those behaviours are documented somewhere and reviewed regularly to ensure that they're still effective and driving the Relationships that you'd like to have in your team. A typical team only needs three to five of these expected behaviours to make a difference. Less is more!

Team members strive consistently to demonstrate expected behaviours in the team

Once you've agreed what the expected behaviours should be in your team, it's then important to ensure that your team members demonstrate and live up to those behaviours. Remember that you're on a journey as a team towards your expected behaviours and sometimes people may lapse. It's human. In those situations it's important to hold people accountable for their behaviours and to move back to expectations and commitments as quickly as possible. If you don't have that conversation, the norm will slip and others will follow. As a foundation skill, you'll need to hold each individual team member accountable for demonstrating these behaviours. It's also important that you, as the leader, role-model these behaviours yourself. If you're not demonstrating them, then how can you expect your team members to do so?

One of the resulting outcomes of people not demonstrating the expected behaviours in the team is what we call 'destructive conflict'. This is when individuals in teams say one thing and do something else. When they undermine and challenge people in a way that's not in service of the positive intent of the team. It's about showing themselves to be better or superior to others or it's about having another agenda and trying to influence the team to do something that's not in service of the team's Reason or Results.

It's also about how team members receive challenge from others. Do team members respond defensively or with anger to comments that are made about their work? Do they feel insulted by others in the team, whether that insult was intended? Is there a sense of competition in the team? Do people feel they need to compete for best position or to be the leader's favourite? All these behaviours aren't helpful or conducive to good Relationships in a team and it's important to ensure that you have a way of managing this kind of conflict when it occurs. Helping your team to notice when it happens and to hold individual team members accountable for the impact they have on other people in the team through their behaviours is essential. It's also crucial that you manage your own reactions to other people's behaviour in your team. This enables you to manage destructive conflict and turn the team culture into one where constructive conflict is possible.

We're not talking about having no conflict in your team. The absence of conflict can be just as destructive as conflict itself. If you have a team that never disagrees, never says a cross word, never gets a bit heated, then we would argue there may well be a problem in your team. A bigger problem than you might realize. A little bit of healthy conflict is a good thing in a team. You just need a strategy for dealing with it when it happens, so that team members can get back to an equilibrium in the team. Conflict is particularly important when teams are stuck. Generating a bit of conflict by sometimes being a bit provocative can be a positive strategy for shifting the team and getting them out of that comfort zone and thinking differently.

Teams often try to avoid the conversation of conflict but we would suggest that it's healthy to talk about what should happen when conflict occurs in your team. What's acceptable and what's not? What happens if a line is crossed? How do team members come back from that? Do they need to apologize to each other? All these things are healthy for helping a team to manage conflict well and to continue their own personal development. Make sure you include something on conflict in your agreed behaviours.

Team members demonstrate reliability-based trust

Trust is an essential part of good Relationships in a team. Trust has two distinct levels. The first is reliability-based trust. This is when team members trust that other team members will do what they said they were going to do. The second is vulnerability-based trust, which is a stretch skill built upon the foundation of reliability-based trust. We'll discuss this later in the context of stretch skills for Relationships.

When you have reliability-based trust, your team members can predict that their colleagues will deliver on their commitments. That they'll deliver a piece of work on time. That they'll be available when they need them to be. This is essential for the foundation of trust in a team. Without it, a team won't be able to rely on each other, so can't work interdependently. Instead, they'll constantly doubt that their colleagues will do what they say they're going to do. They'll question whether other team members will deliver to deadline, give them the support that they need and be available when they need them most. They'll question their colleagues' performance.

So how do you create reliability-based trust in your team? This links back to the expected behaviours in your team. Make sure that when you have that discussion, you include how team members will deliver on their commitments to each other and how they'll hold each other accountable for this. Encourage team members to communicate about commitments with each other openly and to ask questions to explore potential misunderstandings about those commitments. When misunderstandings arise, coach them on what happened and what they could do differently next time.

Team members commit to decisions made by the team

Have you ever come out of a team meeting thinking that you'd made a key decision and everyone agreed? However, have you then found that within a day or two people were acting as if the decision never happened? How frustrating is that? This is a sign that there's a lack of commitment around that decision, which suggests a flaw in the decision-making process you used.

There are two steps to decision-making: gaining agreement and then gaining commitment. Let's look at each of these in turn.

Gaining agreement

It's critical for a high-performing team to be clear on the process you have to gaining agreement for a decision. What often happens in meetings is that teams work based on assumption – this means that if people don't speak up, they assume they agree with what's being said. This is a big mistake. Silence rarely means agreement. In fact, silence can mean many things instead:

- I disagree but don't have the chance/don't want to say so

- I have questions still
- I'm reflecting and considering the options
- I'd like to explore different perspectives
- I have concerns
- I'm not paying attention to what's being said

… and many more.

To gain agreement, your team must first have a process for making decisions. To be effective, this process must be clear on who needs to be involved in the decision and what their contribution will be.

There may be different types of decisions that need to be made in your team. Each will have a different strategy for gaining agreement. Here are a few examples:

A strategic decision
A team needs to make an important strategic decision that has wide-reaching implications across the team and their customers/stakeholders. This requires everyone in the team to input and provide all their different perspectives. They'll need to pay attention to impacts they may not have considered yet. Ultimately the final decision will need to be made by the whole team.

Updating processes
A team wants to review and update their internal processes. One of the team members 'owns' this

process. They need to seek input and understand the implications of changing the process on the relevant members of the wider team. They also need to identify who's impacted, to what extent, and they need to consider how to involve them and gain their agreement to the change. This won't require the whole team to be involved in making the decision but the whole team may need to be informed once the decision has been made.

Workload issues

A member in the team has raised an issue about the workloads within their group. They'd like to discuss this with the wider team to see how the workloads could be shared differently. This may not require the whole team to be involved in making the decision but it would be useful for them to have an awareness of what's going on in the wider team. Here it's about redistributing work across the whole team as the team member is appealing for support and flexibility. A team discussion about how workloads can be redistributed, even temporarily, can highlight where strengths, transferable skills and capacity might be available in the team. This can provide a development opportunity for members of the team. So, what started off as a challenge can become powerful and beneficial for the team.

Gaining commitment

Once a team has agreed on a decision, the team needs to commit to the decision fully. This means that they support the decision, even if they disagree with the final decision that was made by the team. In practice, commitment means that team members will defend a decision both inside and outside the team.

For team members to commit to decisions that the team makes, they need to be able to discuss and pick apart that decision before it's made. This means that the appropriate people need to be involved in some way in sharing their opinion and challenging ideas. Without this involvement, team members may have lingering resentments and doubts that aren't verbalized and considered in the decision-making process. This requires good levels of reliability-based trust and understanding of each other's different personality types.

So often we hear of teams who revisit decisions again and again and they feel incredibly frustrated as a result. They feel like they're going around and around discussing the same things repeatedly when actually the decision wasn't made properly in the first place. A lack of commitment is what causes that repetition of decision-making. Team members sometimes may also have not realized when a discussion on a decision has closed and that it's now time to commit to and execute on the decision that's being made. Sometimes team members believe that the decision is still open for debate. Having clarity that the decision has been made is essential. Teams need a process for doing this. This links to Routines (see Chapter 4).

When somebody disagrees with a decision (which, let's face it, happens!), once it has been made, the worst thing that can happen is that they undermine that decision outside of the team. This is a kind of 'I told you so', passive-aggressive behaviour. If this happens, it's important that both the leader and the team hold the person accountable for their behaviour. It's not acceptable. Make sure that you have something in your expected behaviours about this.

> **Team case study**
> A team we worked with recently decided to implement a sales tool within their organization that would help them manage the Relationships with their customers and track deals to completion. Various organizations had bid to win the contract and there was a close contest between two suppliers. The team had to decide which tool to adopt at significant cost to the business. One person in the team had severe reservations because in another role at a previous organization, she'd experienced a poor implementation of the tool. Rather than complaining about it being a poor decision and waiting for the 'I told you so' moment, she channelled the insights that she'd gained from that experience into lessons learned for the team. She still had reservations but she didn't express them outside of the team. Everyone experienced her full commitment to the decision that the team had made and she worked hard to make it a success. In this example, she was able to commit to the decision because she was part of making it. She was able to voice her opinions and share her experience with the team. The team valued that experience and still decided in favour of that supplier without making the team member feel undervalued or excluded. This is commitment in action.

Stretch skills

These are the skills that will truly take your team to the next level with their Relationships. Your team won't achieve the stretch skills until you've developed the foundation skills.

Team members have vulnerability-based trust

A good team has reliability-based trust, which, as we've established earlier, means that team members do what they say they're going to do. When it comes to a high-performing team, its members have vulnerability-based trust. This is when team members know each other well enough to be able to share what their weaknesses are, where they feel less confident and where they might need help. Team members know that other members of the team will support them if they don't have the skills or experience to complete some new task or if they just don't have all the answers.

To create vulnerability-based trust in your team, you first need to have a foundation of reliability-based trust. It takes time and effort to create vulnerability-based trust and there are many things that you can do within your team to shortcut the process and help them get there quicker.

We often see teams that have individuals who have vulnerability-based trust with one or two other people in the team. The difference between a good and a high-performing team is that in the high-performing team everybody is included in that vulnerability-based trust, even when people are quite different.[17]

Asking people to share a little bit more about who they are as people, as opposed to just focusing on the tasks that

---

[17] On our website you'll find several trust exercises that you can download for free and use in your team: www.management-dynamics.com/leading-edge

they do at work, helps build trust enormously. As with most things in Relationships, this requires continuous investment and it's important to place a renewed focus on it when new people join the team. How do you ensure that new people feel included and valued straightaway and enabled to share who they are with the rest of the team as quickly as possible? Vulnerability-based trust is all about accepting that people aren't perfect and everyone has areas to develop. Creating a learning environment and developmental culture within your team can support the move towards vulnerability-based trust. This requires the leader to have not just 1-2-1 conversations with individuals about their development and their career aspirations but also include a team approach.

Giving feedback directly to each other is also a way to develop vulnerability-based trust as a team. It needs to be done well and we've had some wonderful experiences with teams where they've spent time preparing appreciative and constructive feedback to each other. By the end of it everybody has grown and is in a much stronger place, particularly as they realize how much they're appreciated by everybody and how much support they have.

'You should be able to have a conversation with anyone about anything if you do it in a respectful manner.'

David Allen
Managing Director Pacific and Greater Asia,
Pandora

Team members are willing to admit mistakes

When team members aren't willing to admit their mistakes, they may cover up and hide things that have gone wrong. This means that they and their team can't learn from them. It also reduces the likelihood of them ever taking any risks. Team members will seek a safe way of doing things to minimize the likelihood of making mistakes. Mistakes may only be uncovered when things are going so wrong that they can't be hidden any more, or when the person has left and someone else takes over. This builds distrust in the team.

When you have vulnerability-based trust, you'll find that team members are able and willing to admit their mistakes. They'll proactively share their mistake and their learning from that mistake with the rest of the team. They won't fear that they'll be punished, be humiliated, or that it will be held against them by the rest of the team. This means that team members will be able to take more risks, they'll be willing to try new approaches, tools and ways of working. All of this is the foundation for innovation and creativity in the team. This also develops courage in your team members as they know they can take risks and learn from new experiences.

Team members ask each other for help

When team members aren't able to ask each other for help they may try to carry on regardless, which can be the source of intense personal frustration and can create overwhelm. It can lead to tasks being late or of poor quality. It can also lead to burnout and an inequality of workloads in the team.

In high-performing teams, vulnerability-based trust also results in team members being able to ask each other for help. When you have vulnerability-based trust, people know that they won't be judged by their colleagues if they're struggling with a task or decision. They know that the door will be open for support, brainstorming ideas and sharing resources. When team members ask each other for help, they can also assist each other to grow and develop through sharing knowledge and skills.

Team members constructively challenge each other in service of better outcomes

In a high-performing team, its members regularly respectfully challenge each other. This isn't challenge for the sake of challenge, it's for the sake of creating better decisions and outputs together. This can take the form of constructive challenge – which is asking questions for better understanding. This is when team members deliberately ask questions of what's being presented to challenge thinking, to help people think about different perspectives and to be open to new possibilities. Team members often need permission from each other to do this. It also requires strong levels of trust to avoid team members on the receiving end of this feeling they're under attack and being criticized. Ensure at the start of this process that everybody understands there's a principle of positive intent and that this process is all about improving outcomes for the team. This relies upon the foundation skills being present in the team as well as vulnerability-based trust. Without this level of trust, the likelihood of team members getting defensive and feeling criticized is high.

Team members also need good questioning skills so that things don't get personal. For example, they shouldn't ask, 'Why are you doing this?' as this question can create a defensive response in others. They should ask something like, 'What impact will this idea have on our customers?' This expresses curiosity and exploration. Paying close attention to the words that are used is important in constructive challenge. Here are some core principles to share with your team.

Giving constructive challenge

- Avoid the word 'but' – replace it with 'and' ('but' creates defensiveness as it suggests that you disagree with what has been said).
- When asking questions, start your question with a 'what' or a 'how' (these are open questions that are curious and invite a constructive response) and avoid 'why' questions.
- Don't expect an immediate response or even agreement. If it's a powerful challenge, it will be thought-provoking, which means they'll need time to reflect on it.
- Signal to the other person that you're about to challenge them constructively by saying something like, 'Is it okay if I offer a different perspective?' or 'I'd like to suggest a different point of view,' or 'I'm going to challenge your thinking here.'

Receiving constructive challenge

- Thank people when they constructively challenge you.

- Acknowledge a constructive challenge even if you disagree with it. Say things like, 'That's a good question,' 'That's a powerful insight,' 'I hadn't considered that,' 'That's an interesting perspective.'
- Don't feel like you must respond or agree immediately. If you need time to reflect on it, say so.
- Notice your reaction to the challenge. If you feel yourself getting defensive, consider what's causing this. Remind yourself that the other person has positive intent for the outcome.

Not only is it important to pay attention to the words that team members are using when they constructively challenge each other, it's also important to pay close attention to their tone of voice and body language. The tone of voice should be calm, curious and warm. Body language should be open and relaxed. Change the tone and the meaning shifts. People put much more emphasis on the tone of voice and body language than the words themselves. Help your team to think about what message they're really sending when they say something.

Another way in which constructive challenge can be used in a high-performing team is by the use of the 'devil's advocate' role. This is when team members deliberately take on the role of somebody who sees things very differently from the rest of the team. They can then purposefully challenge from the opposite viewpoint from the team. Team members can find this skill difficult to start with and need practice. Get one team member to play this role at each team meeting and rotate the role around the team so that everyone gets a go eventually. Reflect on what works and what doesn't and how they could play the role even better next time, perhaps by stepping into the shoes of a particularly critical stakeholder for the team.

Team case study

This team wanted to build the skill of constructive challenge in their team. They already had the foundation skills in place and had good levels of vulnerability-based trust. To develop constructive challenge, we introduced the concept of the 'devil's advocate' role in a team meeting. They practised taking turns playing that role throughout the meeting. They found it challenging at first to think differently about the topic at hand and to really stretch their perspective. It helped for them to put themselves in the shoes of their most critical stakeholder to do this. They even started talking as if they were that stakeholder. They realized that by having different perspectives they made better decisions and avoided 'group think'. It really energized their meetings and focused their thinking on the things that really mattered. They now actively have one person playing the role of devil's advocate at each meeting and rotate that role around the team. They fed back to us that playing devil's advocate has on at least one occasion helped them to find a much more effective solution to a significant issue in their business.

Team members proactively include others

Inclusion is important in high-performing teams. Here we're talking about inclusion at its most fundamental level, where all people within the team feel included equally in the activities of the team. This means that they have consistent amounts of airtime in the team, so they get to share their opinions and achievements as much as anybody else in the team. In larger teams, this clearly becomes much harder, as including everybody takes more time the more people there are in the team. It's important to consider how you structure team meetings and how you set up your Routines to ensure that people feel included in key decisions, discussions and activities within the team. Done poorly, inclusive meetings are long, many of the topics are irrelevant to participants and at worst a waste of time.

Inclusion doesn't mean sharing everything with each other in the team all the time, it's about being included in the key moments that matter. It's about being included where you can add real value and feel that you have a contribution to make. Real inclusion is about inviting in the quieter members of the team to the discussion. It's about recognizing that reflective people need time to consider their thoughts before contributing. It's about ensuring that the extroverts in the team stay quiet every now and again and let others speak. It's about actively gathering everyone's point of view to make key decisions. It's about inviting someone to share an opinion even when they have little experience in the topic being discussed. It's about helping people who are less confident in their opinion still to have an opportunity to share some thoughts.

When team members are included in a team, they feel a sense of connection and belonging. They feel that their opinion matters and that they're contributing to the team and making a real difference to their stakeholders and customers. They'll gain confidence to share their opinion even more when they're included. This creates a virtuous circle, where more inclusion means more sharing of opinions, which creates more inclusion and a growing sense of belonging. When people have a strong sense of belonging, it creates huge loyalty for a team.

So, practically, how can you create inclusion in your team? Here are some suggestions.

Decision round
When a key decision needs to be discussed, go round each team member and ask for their opinion on the matter. Ensure that you set some ground rules for this with the team. For example, this could include only speaking when it's your turn; no judgement of anyone's opinion; there's no such thing as a bad idea; if you want to refer to anyone's suggestion, present it as a 'build' question, only for clarification/understanding.

Another way of doing this is to get each person to write a thought about the decision on a sticky note and put it up on a board/wall. Then discuss the ideas.

To use this tool to finalize a decision, go round each person and ask whether they're 'for' or 'against' the proposed action. Each person should explain their position, with no judgement or argument from other team members.

Team coaching questions
If no decision needs to be made and you just want to promote discussion and reflection in the team, you could use some

team coaching questions. Get each person to choose a question at random, then each person answers their question in turn. Make sure everyone gets a go.[18]

Opinion-seeker role
Have a role called the 'opinion seeker', which gets rotated around the team. This person's role is to keep an eye on the quieter people in the team and to invite them into the conversation every now and again. Introverts will often wait to be invited into a conversation and this role makes sure that their voices and opinions are heard. The kind of things you might say/ask are, 'X, I notice you've been very quiet in this meeting – what do you think of this?' or 'I'd love to hear X's view on this...'

Create projects to promote collaboration
Sometimes you might have a team that's not very interdependent, so their roles are quite separate and independent of each other. They might be able to get their work done without relying on any other team member. When this happens, it can be useful to use collaboration to create a sense of inclusion in the team. For example, you could get team members working on a project together deliberately so that they create a feeling of belonging. You could also get team members to share best practices or what they're working on with the wider team. Again, this will create that sense of inclusion and contribution for them.

Induct new team members
When new people join the team, it's important to include them as early as possible in team activities and share their expertise

---

[18] You can find some example team coaching questions on our website: www.management-dynamics.com/leading-edge

and transferable skills with the team. This is particularly important when people are working remotely and is a way of connecting them very quickly to others who they may not have the opportunity to build a Relationship with otherwise.

Going the extra mile

When Relationships are poor in a team, people become much more selfish and will focus mainly on their own tasks and objectives. They may not even notice when other people in the team are struggling. The last thing they're thinking about is helping others.

When Relationships are good in a team, people will go the extra mile for their team members. They'll try harder, they'll support each other more and they'll be available to give advice to each other when it's needed. They notice when they can help and they want to offer their support. Their commitment to the team and the team's Reason is greater. This means that they'll sacrifice their own personal goals and agenda for the good of the team. People get a huge sense of contribution and well-being when conditions enable them to do this.

Avoid forced fun

Social activities are helpful in building Relationships in a team. Spending time together outside of work is a powerful tool for breaking down barriers, building trust and getting to know each other at a fun, more fundamental level. However, it must be done well, in an inclusive way and must consider a whole range of factors that might impact the individuals in the team in different ways. We would suggest that forcing people to have fun doesn't build Relationships and what's perceived as fun by one person in the team might not be shared by somebody else. For example, some people in the team may find a team human table football game fun, but when one team member has mobility issues it's excluding for them.

Ensure that everyone is happy to take part in social activities and that the timing works for everyone. Team members who have children may find evening/weekend events hard to attend. Asking people to stay out very late may impact the team member with a long commute. The key is to ask people's opinions and to make social events optional. Observe who attends and who doesn't. Those who don't attend will feel excluded even if it was their choice not to attend. The point is not to stop all social events, it's about choosing events that can be inclusive of everyone in the team. Or it may be a mix of events that can include the whole team over time. Or maybe you need to do something during the working day. Talk to the team and involve them in idea generation.

Relationship diagnostic

As we've already established, Relationships are complex, and you may wonder where to start first. To help you with this we've created a Relationship assessment, which you'll find on our website.[19] You can use it to assess your team against the dimensions of Relationships in teams – both foundation and stretch skills. This will help you to identify where to start with your team.

---

[19] www.management-dynamics.com/leading-edge

The links to other Edge Dynamics

Relationships are the glue that determines how it feels to be a part of this team, which is a crucial element of performance. Let's explore how Relationships link to the other Edge Dynamics.

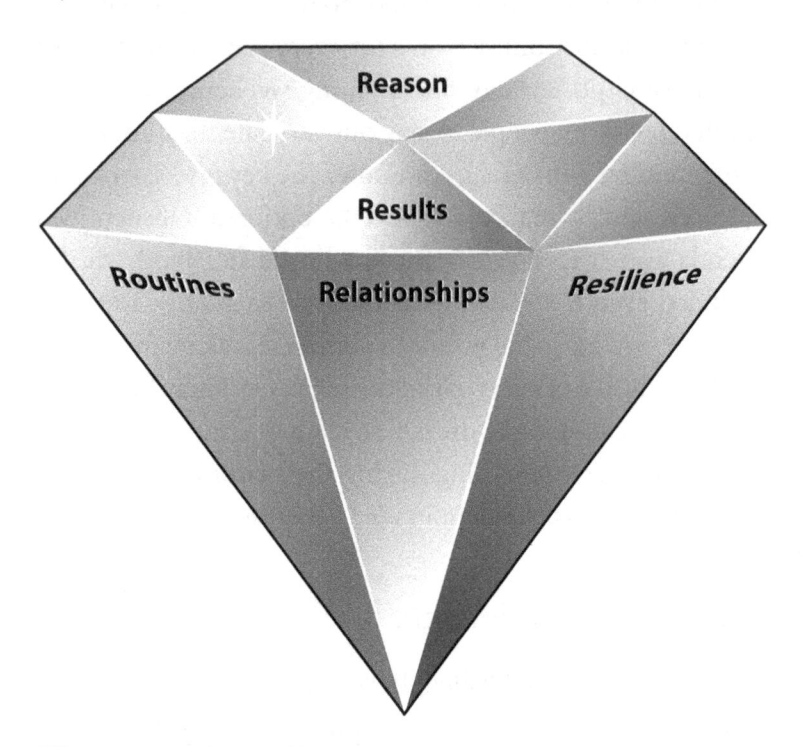

The connection to Reason

By working on Relationships in a team you're helping the team to get closer to what their own individual Reason is and therefore what the team Reason might be (see Chapter 2). Often, when we work with teams, team members share their personal work values with the team and notice the similarities and differences between their personal values. Values are a crucial part of who we are and what motivates us at work. They're also a foundation of Relationships. When team members understand each other's values, it builds Relationships and helps them manage destructive conflict. Here you're effectively killing two birds with one stone and working on both Reason and Relationships at the same time. Relationships in teams create a sense of connection and belonging, and when we look at people's values in teams, we often see those words popping up. Connection and belonging are an important motivator for a lot of people. As are things like trust, honesty, integrity and making a difference.

When you look at teams' expected behaviours, you also often see a direct connection back to the team Reason. By working with the team on their expected behaviours, you're reinforcing and deepening the Reason your team exists.

The connection to Results

When you work on Relationships in a team you're providing the conditions for success in the team's Results (see Chapter 3). You're enabling them to work together well on shared team objectives. You're providing the foundation for collaboration in the team and the sharing of ideas and best practice. This enables innovation, creativity and better problem-solving in your team. The team is able to deal with complexity much more effectively as their Relationships give them the courage and the edge they need to face things head-on.

You're also enabling people in your team to deliver superior Results at the individual level because they can share ideas, learn new skills from other members of the team and receive mentoring. This creates confidence at the individual level, which means that they'll be more likely to take risks and try new things. All these things together enable superior Results in your team.

The connection to Routines

When you work on Relationships in your team, very quickly any gaps in your Routines (see Chapter 4) will become obvious. Identify the Routines that cause friction in the team – either because they're perceived to be wasting people's time, because they're not inclusive of all team members or they're not in service of Results or Reason. Very quickly the team will see which Routines promote the behaviours that the team doesn't want to see. It will be important to adjust those Routines straightaway to enable the behaviours that you want to see as a team. Consider how your Routines strengthen and enable Relationships in your team and where they get in the way or at worst undermine them completely.

Beginnings and endings are important in teams, so make sure that you have Routines specifically around inducting new people into the team. This might include updating the team's values when a new team member joins, working out who they need to collaborate with or discussing how they can work well together. It's also important to ensure that it's not a one-way process when inducting a new person. Relationships are two-way, so team members should be curious about the new person, their experience and skills and also about what they're like as a person to work with. They should also be generous in sharing their own experience, skills and how they like to work most effectively.

Leaving is also a critical process. It's important to ensure that people leave the team with a feeling of goodwill, appreciation and a readiness to succeed in the future. The remaining team members need to feel this too. Having a Routine when somebody leaves is essential and is more than just handing over tasks and making sure their projects or activities are in a good state. Just as important, it's about valuing that person and sharing some appreciative, constructive feedback of what they brought to the team. It's about enabling the team to wish them well going forward, and vice versa. A lovely example of this occurred while we were away writing this book as one of our team members was due to leave that week. We arranged a team meeting on their last day. Each person delivered some appreciative feedback to the person leaving. The person was then able to respond back with what they'd really appreciated about working with each of the individuals in the team as well as the team as a whole. It was a great ending for our Relationships with the team member.

The connection to Resilience

When you work on Relationships in your team, you're, by default, also working on Resilience (see Chapter 6). Resilience relies on strong Relationships. Humans are designed to be part of a community and at work the team is their community. The team needs good Relationships to have that sense of community support, so if you need your team to be more resilient, look at their Relationships. Where are they weak and where do they need to be strengthened?

Isolation and exclusion in a team undermines team members' Resilience. Thinking about how you create a sense of belonging, connection and inclusion in your team is essential for building Resilience. Relationships enable team members to share their mistakes, knowledge and skills. They also enable a supportive environment when mistakes are made that builds the ability to bounce back from setbacks.

'Relationships are needed to sustain long-term business performance.'

Frederic Debrosses
General Manager, Middle East, Africa,
Global Business Development, JDE Peet's

Relationships – a summary

Relationships interlink with the Edge Dynamics of Routines and Resilience to support *how* the team operates. Without effective Relationships, a team is not a team – they're just a bunch of people who all happen to work for the same boss. Relationships are, in essence, the interactions between the individuals in a team and how much value those interactions bring to the team and the achievement of their Results and Reason.

We've identified several key skills that teams need to develop to be truly high-performing when it comes to their Relationships. They're divided into two levels: the foundation skills that team members need to have good solid Relationships, and what we call the stretch skills that will truly take your team to the next level. Your team won't achieve the stretch skills until you've developed the foundation skills.

Foundation skills:

- Team members understand each other and have mutual respect

- Team members are clear about what expected behaviours are in the team
- Team members strive consistently to demonstrate expected behaviours in the team
- Team members demonstrate reliability-based trust
- Team members commit to decisions made by the team

Stretch skills:

- Team members have vulnerability-based trust
- Team members are willing to admit mistakes
- Team members ask each other for help
- Team members constructively challenge each other in the service of better outcomes
- Team members proactively include others in the team in meetings and events

When Relationships are good in a team, people will go the extra mile for their team members. Social activities are helpful in building Relationships in a team. Spending time together outside of work is a powerful tool for breaking down barriers, building trust and getting to know each other at a fun, more fundamental level. However, 'forced fun' should be avoided – include team members in defining what social activities take place and how to include everyone.

CHAPTER 6

Resilience

Continuously review the Edge Dynamics in your team. Maintain your team's energy, motivation and endurance for high performance. Know what to look out for and the signs that things need to be adjusted in the team, enabling them to flex and adjust to change.

What is team Resilience?

Resilience is a person's ability to bounce back from adversity. In a team context, the same definition applies, we just extend it a bit and change the emphasis from bouncing back to bouncing forward – when team members support each other to come back from adversity even stronger than before.

A team is made up of a group of individuals and each person has their own level of Resilience. When team members collaborate with each other, meet with each other or interact in some way, team Resilience also becomes important.

If people are excluded (or exclude themselves), don't collaborate and so on, then that will reduce the Resilience of both the individuals and the team more widely. Low Resilience is infectious. We can infect others with our state of mind unintentionally.

One of the gaps in teams is that leaders often think about individuals within the team only and how they're doing, and don't tap into the power of the team to create Resilience. Resilience is also infectious in a positive way – the strength of one individual's Resilience can lift that of another team member. And the team also contributes to individual Resilience – teams provide many of the solutions to Resilience – connection, support, contribution, fulfilment of values and many more things that all build up our Resilience.

When people talk about Resilience, they usually consider it through one of two viewpoints: either individual Resilience or organizational Resilience. We would argue that team Resilience is also an essential viewpoint for creating high performance. Let's explore each of these in turn.

Individual Resilience

According to the American Psychological Association, individual Resilience 'is the process and outcome of successfully adapting to difficult or challenging life experiences, especially through mental, emotional, and behavioural flexibility and adjustment to external and internal demands.'[20] When someone has Resilience, when challenges occur, instead of demonstrating unhealthy coping strategies (or just not coping), people are able to face difficulties head-on.

Organizational Resilience

Organizational Resilience is the ability of an organization to withstand crises, unexpected events and disruptions to their

---

[20] www.apa.org/topics/resilience

business through unforeseen circumstances. There are plenty of good examples, such as pandemics, geopolitical tensions, financial market disruption and supply chain issues. A resilient organization plans for the unexpected, actively manages its cashflow and reserves and adapts its business quickly to the changing environment. A resilient organization is constantly looking to the future to try to anticipate future challenges and plan a response.

Team Resilience

The critical link between individual and organizational Resilience is *team* Resilience. When you have good Resilience in your team, it provides Resilience into the organization through anticipation of challenge and change in their area. They also assist individuals with their own personal Resilience by providing support, adjustment of workloads and ways of working. This is the key to sustaining high performance over time. If organizations want to truly be resilient, they need to focus on building team Resilience, and yet it's so often overlooked. Many organizations have put in place excellent well-being programmes and support, which is all about supporting individual Resilience. The impact of these efforts would be magnified if more of an emphasis was placed on the links into team Resilience.

For your team to be resilient, the team members need to plan how they're going to shift and change to new requirements that come in. As new members join and people leave, they need to think about how they learn from their activities and projects and incorporate that learning into future work that they do. The team needs to grow and develop so that they're ready to take on new tasks, be innovative and creative and also to ensure the personal growth of each individual within the team.

If a team doesn't have strong Resilience, yet has high levels of all the other Edge Dynamics, there's no way they can be truly high-performing. They won't sustain any performance levels they achieve for very long, and a high-performing team gets to high performance and maintains it over time. This Edge Dynamic more than any other is the one that teams pay little attention to, yet it's the one that will enable the team to sustain high performance. This is the key to reaping all the benefits of high engagement. In a resilient team, people feel satisfied in their jobs and deliver incredible Results.

Team Resilience isn't just about managing what's right in front of you and being able to bounce forward from setbacks. It's also about being able to anticipate changes and challenges on the horizon and adjust your team's response. It's about preparing for and being proactive about changes that are about to come along in the short, medium and long term.

What do high-performing, resilient teams do?

High-performing, resilient teams:

- Do more with what they have
- Work smarter not harder
- Take proper breaks
- Celebrate the small wins
- Laugh together
- Believe there's only winning and learning

Do more with what they have

High-performing teams are able to make the most of the resources that they have and stretch beyond what they previously thought was possible to do even more. They don't necessarily need to ask for more resources. They challenge themselves to think outside the box instead.

Work smarter not harder

They work in smarter ways rather than harder. High-performing teams look for ways to work more efficiently rather than taking on more work. This increases their capacity for greater things. They continuously review and remove Routines that no longer add value.

Take proper breaks

They understand how important it is to take regular, proper breaks that enable team members to recharge and recuperate. They encourage and assist team members in taking breaks and ensure that they're true breaks from the work without interruption. This includes breaks throughout the working day as well as vacation time.

Celebrate the small wins

They continuously celebrate the little milestones that, added together, make up big achievements. They know that this is a key to sustaining motivation over long periods of time. They also celebrate individual successes as a reflection on the team.

Laugh together

High-performing teams have fun and enjoy working together, even when the work they do is high stakes. They laugh regularly and seek out moments of fun.

Believe there's only winning and learning

They don't believe in 'failure' as a concept – they see this as an opportunity to learn and do even better next time. In this way there's only winning and learning.

The impact of Resilience on sustaining high performance

When teams have low levels of Resilience, they can struggle to sustain high performance over a long period of time. Team members get exhausted, may burn out or lose interest in the work and seek other opportunities outside of the team. If you have high levels of turnover in your team or lots of absence or sickness, we would argue that you've probably got low levels of Resilience. Nearly every team scores lowest on Resilience the first time they run our Advantycs® diagnostic. Most teams pay little attention to Resilience, compared to the other Edge Dynamics. They may review workloads in the team and encourage team members to manage their own individual Resilience but this is usually as far as it goes and they don't harness the power of the team. Only the best teams pay really close attention to actively managing Resilience at the team level.

When teams have high levels of Resilience, they're capable of sustaining high performance over long periods of time. This means they can deliver at the highest levels, continuously. The whole team is committed to supporting other team members to deliver superior outcomes. This means working together to manage the energy of the whole team, not just the individuals within it. The team sets a pace and adapts it so that they can sustain that level of high performance for everyone.

When one person's energy levels are low in the team, the rest of the team adapts, supporting them to re-energize and adjusting workload to ensure Results are still delivered.

High-performing teams sustain high performance over time largely due to the fact that they're continuously learning. They pay close attention to what works and what doesn't and are curious about finding new ways to deliver Results. They're always asking, 'How can that be done differently?' They use collaboration to simplify complex issues and to come up with innovative solutions together. The emphasis is always on 'us' as a team rather than 'me' as an individual. This means that the burden of Results is shared across the team. Individual team members benefit enormously from this as there are massive opportunities for personal growth, supported by the whole team.

The power of substitution

When we talk to teams, we often hear about the adrenaline and satisfaction that team members can get from a burst of energy around a particular deliverable. However, it's hard to maintain that level of output over a long period of time. People need rest and recuperation to have the energy that they need to deliver at that level again. This is where the power of the team can really make a difference. When an individual tries to sustain prolonged periods of high output, they invariably can't do it for long. Physically, humans need regular breaks. In a high-performing team, there's no need for a reduction in team performance because team members can substitute for each other. They can plan in breaks and rest time for physical, mental and emotional recharge. This means that the overall performance of the team is sustained and each individual gets time to recuperate and be ready to perform back at high levels again. In team sports, we see this happening all the time. Teams use substitutes to bring players on and off the pitch to compensate for a drop in energy levels of players who've been on the pitch for a while. Sometimes the team might also need a different skill for that stage of the game – for example, when penalties are looking likely in soccer, teams may bring on their best penalty takers as substitutes.

Why not take this concept and bring it into your team? Think about how to substitute your key players when they need a break or specialist skills are required. Substitution requires good levels of collaboration, great Relationships (Chapter 5), efficient Routines (Chapter 4), excellent clarity of Reason (Chapter 2) and a laser-like focus on Results (Chapter 3). In fact, all the other Edge Dynamics contribute to enabling substitution to happen.

Flow

When a team has high levels of Resilience, the concept of flow becomes possible more often in the team.[21] A flow state, or 'being in the zone', is the mental state in which people feel fully immersed in what they're doing. They lose all concept of time, are fully focused, deeply concentrating on the work at hand and are really energized by it. Teams can get into a flow state too when they're collaborating, brainstorming and working on things together really well. High-performing teams regularly get into flow. People don't want to leave teams where this happens often.

---

[21] M. Csíkszentmihályi, *Flow* (2002).

Resilience by design

We know, by working with hundreds of teams, that Resilience doesn't happen by chance – it has to happen by design. There are multiple elements fundamental to building a team's Resilience and it's a continuous process. In sport, teams train over time to build up their endurance, their speed and their strength. They practise playing different positions in the team so that they can substitute for each other in times of injury or exhaustion. They develop deep expertise in specific skills required in the team, and a team will never rely on just one person to have those skills. How can you use this idea within your team? How do you design and develop your team for Resilience? Resilience isn't something that can be done 'to' a team, it's something that you need to design 'with' them, involving them in the process. Team Resilience will also vary from team to team, so it's important to find strategies and ways of working that are effective for the personalities and needs of the people within your team.

Single points of failure

Most teams that we work with have single points of failure. This means that they have critical tasks and skills that can only be done by one person in the team. When that person takes a vacation, is off sick or absent for any reason, that task doesn't get done. This is okay if you can plan around periods of absence but sometimes they happen unexpectedly or are long term.

Single points of failure can also result in a team member feeling overloaded before they go on vacation as they try to prepare for their time off and to not be overwhelmed when they come back and try to clear the backlog that has built up in their absence. They may be tempted to check their emails regularly while they're away to keep that particular task ticking over, so that when they come back they don't have so much backlog to clear. This means that they're not truly getting the mental break they need from work to be refreshed on their return.

Sometimes you might find one team member who's unwilling to share their knowledge and skills. They might not want to help develop a substitute in the team. This may be because their sense of status as an expert in the team might be threatened. They may also get a huge sense of security knowing that they're the only person in the team who can complete the task and that they're indispensable. It's essential to address this. Make it clear that it's unacceptable for them to put their own needs above the needs of the team. They need to play the role of mentor in the team in order for the team to achieve their Results with minimal risk. They can also continue to develop their own skills by being a substitute for other people's areas of responsibility.

High-performing teams have no single points of failure in the team. This means that they don't rely on one person to do a particular task all the time. They know what the critical tasks are and they invest in developing multiple people to do those tasks well. This includes some of the tasks that are carried out by the leader. A high-performing team can sustain performance without a leader for some time but this doesn't mean they can do it forever. At a minimum, a team should be able to perform without contacting you while you're on vacation. Think about what your single points of failure might be. Who currently has the skills to substitute and cover those single points of failure if an individual were to be off sick or away for some reason? Who might benefit from developing those skills?

Create a culture of learning

People often think of Resilience as bouncing *back* from setbacks. As we said earlier, we prefer to think of it as bouncing *forward*. This means they don't just revert back to how they used to do things, they learn from the experience and they've developed as result. They're stronger in some way. In high-performing teams this also happens. When a setback occurs, the team bounces *forward*, having learned from experiences and they challenge themselves to stretch and adapt. High-performing teams invite challenge, which creates adaptation and learning without a setback needing to occur. They're then ready when setbacks do happen. There are numerous key things that high-performing teams should pay attention to when seeking to create a culture of experimentation and learning. This includes developing an agile mindset, experimentation, changing perspectives and holding up the mirror. Let's look at each in turn.

Agile mindset

An agile mindset is one where all team members are open to looking at what they do as individuals as well as challenging how other team members are doing things. They look externally for new ways of operating – they're not afraid of trying to see the world in a different way and they learn from all types of experiences and influences. It's a mindset of 'can do' and 'how can we do this differently or better?' It's a fundamental belief that anything is possible. As a team this is hugely empowering. An individual team member might lack confidence in one thing but as a team they know that everything is possible – the key is just to find the way.

Experimentation

Teams that have a regular practice of experimenting with how they do things are substantially more successful than teams that don't. Teams that experiment regularly aren't interested in perfection first time. They accept that each time they have a go they're learning from that experience. It's more about the information they gain as they experiment to build towards whatever the final output or outcome might be. All the big leaps in humankind, whether it be reaching the moon or developing a vaccine, have taken an experimentation approach. This is where people learn in small steps and build on what they understand each time. There's no fear or criticism of failure in this process. It's all about what information they're gaining to help them build on being more effective next time and having another go.

High-performing teams use an experimentation mindset approach in everything they do. They use it in how they deal with customers and practise different communication styles to see what will work. They use it in constantly challenging the tools that they use and how those tools could be improved. This doesn't mean that they go messing around with processes and ways of doing things all the time. They experiment in a controlled way with permission from the rest of the team. They have a Routine for reflecting on what works and what doesn't, for planning experiments and managing the risks associated with that. They review the results of their experiments and then decide what to do next. How could your team experiment more? What conditions would you need to put in place to enable that to happen?

Changing perspective

High-performing teams don't just have one way of looking at things. They regularly change their perspective to see things differently and to notice things that they might not have spotted otherwise. They create Routines that help them to change their perspective on their work. They talk to people outside the team to get different viewpoints and they identify experiences that will create insights and connections. These experiences don't need to be directly related to the work of the team to be successful. In fact, the more different they are the better. The most important thing is to be able to explore the analogy that the experience creates and bring that back into the team as learning. We often see teams having enjoyable team-building days or social activities but they're usually isolated events with no link back to the team's day-to-day activities. They may be fun activities but the power of the perspective that could be generated isn't harnessed and brought back into the overall team.

Analogies are incredibly powerful ways to change a team's perspective. What analogies could you use to help your team to think about how they could see their work from another perspective? When you're doing team-building activities, ensure that you always do a debrief of the insights people have created about the team as a result.

Holding up the mirror

While looking outside the team really helps to get a wider perspective, the team also needs to look inside regularly. We call this 'holding up the mirror'. This is about creating experiences that help the team to reflect on how it's working and what could be improved. It's also about helping the team to see how well they're demonstrating their expected behaviours and where they could create further opportunities from all the difference and diversity within the team.

As team coaches, we often help teams to hold up the mirror. We do this by creating team challenges and by doing team observations. Any experience that's designed to help them notice the dynamics within the team is useful. Using our diagnostic tool is also a way of holding up the mirror. Feedback processes can be a very powerful way for both individual and team development. This means helping your team to give each other feedback on what works and what doesn't in their Relationships with each other. High-performing teams build in Routines to regularly hold the mirror up for themselves and we know when they've got to high performance because they no longer need us to help them with this.

> *'In a fast-paced environment, it's critical to take time out together, gain perspective and share feedback. Understand what impact you are having on each other. Challenge everyone to adapt and to lead the whole team.'*
>
> **Erik Schmidt**
> **Former CHRO, Pandora**

Beginnings and endings

High-performing teams aren't static; they're dynamic. Members of the team will leave at some point and move on to greater things, and new members will join. This is unavoidable and essential for the renewal of the team. Every time someone leaves or joins, the team changes fundamentally – in fact, they become a new team. When a team changes like this, Resilience can drop as the dynamics in the team are impacted. New team members require more support, don't have the same level of clarity as existing team members, don't have the same depth of Relationships and need different Routines to induct them into the team's ways of working. They also need to establish a close connection to the team's Reason. When someone leaves a team, they take their knowledge, skills, energy, passion and Relationships with them. This loss creates a shift in the dynamics in the team, which needs to be discussed and addressed. The team needs to determine how to fill the gaps left behind in such a way that new, productive team dynamics are created.

Endings

Considering how you celebrate endings and capture the knowledge and experience of team members as they leave is critical. This is about ensuring that they leave a legacy behind and don't create a critical failure point in the team by leaving with all that knowledge and experience without it having been captured first. Leaving is more than just the farewell party. Think about all the other things that need to happen when somebody leaves to ensure that it's done well.

We talked in Chapter 5 about the experience of saying farewell to one of our key team members while we were in the process of writing this book. The person leaving focused, in their last few weeks, on documenting their knowledge and skills and on creating the induction plan for their replacement. There was no period of overlap between them. However, they've spoken with their replacement and shared some key insights and top tips for how they can be successful in the role and in the team.

Beginnings

Inducting new members into the team is also critical. How do you bring them in and share with them what the team does, while at the same embracing their fresh perspective on the team? How can you build a Routine to learn from the experience and ideas of people who are joining the team before they become assimilated into the team? You have a short window of opportunity for this – probably no more than three months. High-performing teams look forward to new members joining because they relish the challenge of adapting and becoming a refreshed high-performing team.

The experience of good endings and positive beginnings is crucial for the system that your team is part of. When endings are done poorly, the echoes of that person remain in the system and can last for years. Some teams can also carry the pain of the disappearing individual for a long time, especially when someone just vanishes from the team and there was no opportunity to say goodbye properly. In this situation, rumours and speculation will occur as to what happened to that person. Dealing with it well ensures that you can manage the experience of the team so that it's a good one. It's also about making sure that you're not creating a critical point of failure. A good ending will ensure that the leaver's information, knowledge and skills are handed over well. Often when somebody leaves a team the team or leader are in a hurry to move on and think about the future without them. We've seen many examples of people leaving teams and in their last few days and weeks they're completely excluded from the team. Holding the leaver accountable for creating a positive legacy and impact on the team is essential, while at the same time being accountable yourself for enabling a good ending for that person. It's worth taking the time to ensure that their ending happens well and the beginning of your new team is a positive one. You may feel frustrated that you've invested time and effort developing the person who's leaving but it's worth also noticing what opportunities come from their departure. Someone leaving is always an opportunity to refresh the team.

The lowest-scoring Edge Dynamic

When we run a first diagnostic for a team, 99% of the time Resilience is the lowest-scoring Edge Dynamic. When we consider why that might be, there are several causes. First of all, Resilience is often an afterthought at the team level – if it's considered at all. Teams are unlikely to look at Resilience beyond thinking about it at the individual level. There may be many resources available within the organization that support individuals in the team to manage and develop their own personal Resilience. In our experience, it's very unusual for teams to think about Resilience together and how to utilize the power of the team to strengthen it. When we first start working with teams, usually team members think about themselves first and the team second. This erodes Resilience and means that team members often don't even notice when their colleagues are struggling. They're certainly not anticipating change and having to identify critical pain points and how the team might need to adapt in the future. Team members who are in this frame of mind are often stuck in the weeds of their own work. This means that they're embroiled in the detail and don't even notice what's going on around them. When they start to shift their focus from 'me' to 'we', the impacts on Resilience are immediate.

For all of this to happen, vulnerability-based trust is essential. We know that teams need to build reliability-based trust first and that vulnerability-based trust comes later, once that foundation is in place (see Chapter 5). For there to be strong levels of Resilience in a team, team members need to be able to ask for help, admit they've made mistakes and offer support to others in the team when they need it. They also need to feel comfortable challenging each other and accepting challenge in return. It can be tempting in a team when they get that first diagnostic back to want to start with Resilience – especially when it's the lowest-scoring Edge Dynamic. We would suggest this is a mistake and that investing in Resilience when the other Edge Dynamics are low is like pushing water uphill in a team. Start with the other Edge Dynamics first and resist the temptation to invest lots of time and effort in developing Resilience in your team yet. Doing things in this order will mean that Resilience will improve naturally and the foundation skills will be in place for Resilience to happen. When you then focus on Resilience more deliberately, with strong Edge Dynamics already in place, high performance will be sustainable.

Pay attention to your team's Resilience

As a leader, a key role for you is to pay attention and to notice the Resilience levels of both the members within your team and the team as a whole. This requires keen observation skills. It means being able to notice what people are like when everything is going well, what behaviours they demonstrate and also noticing what people are like when they're under pressure or when the stress levels are high. This calibration of the differences will enable you to notice the indications that team members are struggling. It will help you to ask key questions about their strategies for managing their Resilience and also what the team can do to support them. There are three key energy levels you can pay attention to: physical, mental and emotional.

Your body has varying levels of physical energy depending on the day, the time of day and so on. This can affect both your mental energy, which is your thinking capacity, and your emotional energy, which is your emotional capacity. Have you noticed that if you've worked hard all day long with few breaks, by 9 o'clock at night you find it hard to finish a sentence or to do simple maths? That's your mental energy dropping. And this is something that changes day to day, but our mental and emotional energy can really be impacted by long-term poor physical energy. There's a limit. Or you might find that you take things personally more easily. That's your emotional energy dropping. Let's look at each of the energies in turn, their symptoms and some causes of low energy levels:

Physical energy		
Symptoms	**Causes**	**Possible solutions**
Tiredness Headaches Illness Inability to refresh after breaks	Poor diet to manage the 'dips' Lack of exercise Lack of good-quality sleep Underlying illness Poor boundaries between work and 'time off' Too much screen time Lack of breaks	Review your team Routines – are they fit for purpose? Think about things like: • Walking meetings • Team exercise challenges • Agree team boundaries around working/meeting hours • Team lunches
Mental energy		
Symptoms	**Causes**	**Possible solutions**
Trouble thinking Struggling to see the bigger picture Missing deadlines Finding problem-solving hard Forgetfulness	Poor boundaries between work and 'time off' Overwhelm Lack of focus/prioritization Low physical energy Working for long periods of time without a break	Review your team Reason and Results – are they clear/compelling enough? Help people prioritize workload Discuss workloads at team meetings – are team members' accountabilities

Making mistakes Struggling to deal with change	Working in isolation for too long Lack of variety Spending too much time in the detail	aligned with the team Results? Remind the team of the bigger picture and your team Reason Build in some fun and variety Encourage collaboration Encourage learning new things

Emotional energy

Symptoms	Causes	Possible solutions
More conflicts/ disagreements Struggling to express emotions Taking things personally Lower capacity for creativity and innovation Lack of empathy	Low physical energy Personal values being undermined/ unfulfilled Being in conflict with others Being left out/ isolated – lack of connection with others Not feeling valued by others in team	Work on the team's Relationships – build vulnerability-based trust as a team Create a team contract – how will you behave together? Encourage collaboration and inclusion Help people feel valued, encourage team members to voice this

| Lower confidence
Reluctance to collaborate | Mindset – negative self-talk and making assumptions

Monotony/boredom | Manage the mindset of team members – build confidence

Create variety and fun

Celebrate success |

Role-modelling Resilience

As a leader, your team members follow what you do, not what you say. If you're on your email 24 hours a day and rarely take a proper break, your team will do the same. No matter how much you tell them that breaks are important and that they're not expected to look at their emails outside of working hours, if you do this, they will too. You need to role-model the behaviours you'd like to see in your team. Think about how you behave and the impact it's having on your team.

One leader of a team that we've worked with demonstrated poor Resilience behaviours with his team, which had a massive negative impact on the team. He was constantly interrupting their work to divert their attention to other things. He would phone them on their vacations with questions. And he would contact people at all hours. This meant that the team felt that they were expected to be available all the time and could never truly relax when they weren't working. Unsurprisingly, Resilience was very low in this team. The leader was shocked by the insight that he was part of the cause. People were leaving the team, and absence due to stress was high. He was reducing the team's capacity for performance rather than increasing it. Consider whether your behaviours are enabling your team to be resilient or getting in their way.

The links to other Edge Dynamics

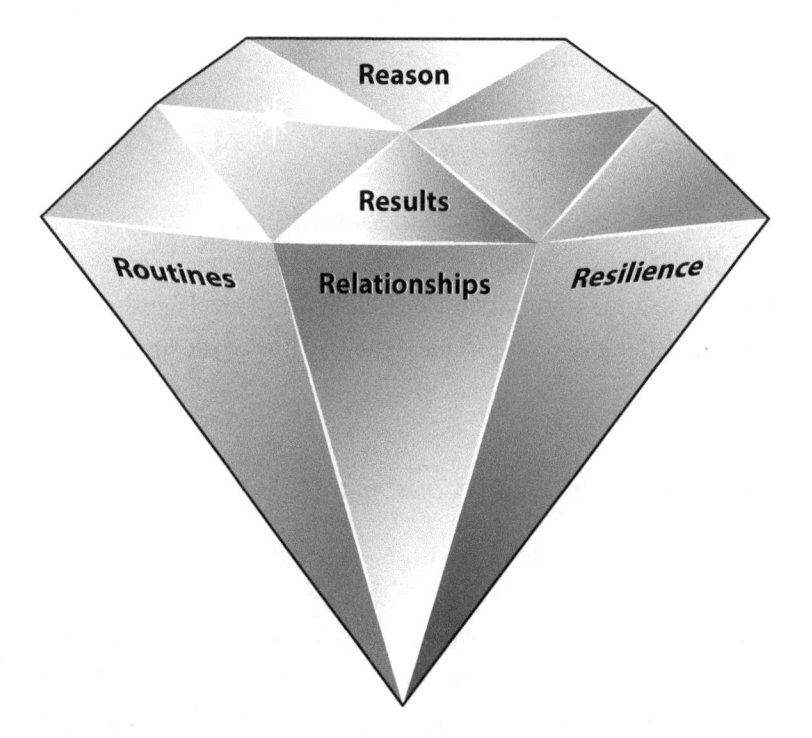

Resilience is affected by all the other Edge Dynamics and, as we've noted, is often the lowest-scoring Edge Dynamic within a team when we first start working with them. All the other Edge Dynamics need to be strong for there to be high levels of Resilience in a team. There are also specific impacts back to the other Edge Dynamics that are worth paying attention to.

The connection to Reason

When Resilience is high in a team, the team will find it easy to tap into their own personal *why* as well as the team's Reason. They'll be more easily motivated and energized and will have the space to maintain line of sight between the work they're doing and the team's purpose. The team uses their Reason to maintain Resilience in tough times.

The connection to Results

High levels of Resilience undoubtedly lead to excellent Results at both the individual and team level. When your team is seamlessly managing their energy levels and anticipated challenges, Results come easily. They work smarter, not harder.

The connection to Relationships

When team Resilience is high, team members feel lower levels of stress – in fact they'd describe stress as motivating them to overcome challenges. It has become a positive force for the team. This means that they have the mental and emotional capacity to build and maintain Relationships with their colleagues. Relationships are strengthened by overcoming challenges together.

The connection to Routines

Teams that have strong levels of Resilience have great Routines. The two go hand in hand and influence each other. High-performing teams are constantly learning and responding to change and this leads to adjusting and adapting Routines regularly to ensure that they're still fit for purpose.

> **Resilience – a summary**
>
> Resilience is the team's ability to support each other to bounce forward from adversity even stronger than before. Resilience interacts with Relationships and Routines to support *how* the team operates. Team Resilience is the key to both individual and organizational Resilience and is fundamental for sustaining high performance over long periods of time.
>
> High-performing, resilient teams:
>
> - Do more with what they have
> - Work smarter not harder
> - Take proper breaks
> - Celebrate the small wins
> - Laugh together
> - Believe there's only winning and learning
>
> If you have high levels of turnover in your team, lots of absence or sickness, we would argue that you've probably got low levels of Resilience. Only the best teams pay close attention to actively managing Resilience at the team level.
>
> Use the idea of substitution to maintain Resilience in your team and allow proper breaks from work without productivity dropping.
>
> Resilience doesn't happen by chance, it has to happen by design. Involve your team in the design of your Routines

with Resilience in mind. Find strategies and ways of working that are effective for the personalities and needs of the people within your team.

Pay attention to the single points of failure in your team. Which critical tasks and skills can only be done by one person in the team? When they're absent, what happens?

Create a culture of learning in your team by developing an agile mindset and creating the conditions for experimentation. Help your team members to change their perspective regularly and hold up the mirror by getting them to notice the dynamics in the team.

Beginnings and endings are crucial for Resilience, so help your team to manage new starters and people leaving the team well.

Pay attention to your team's three energies:

- Physical
- Mental
- Emotional

Role-model Resilience behaviours yourself, as your team pays more attention to what you do than what you say.

PART TWO
Leadership and team development

CHAPTER 7

Leading a high-performing team

In this chapter, we explore:

- The role of the leader in creating and sustaining a high-performing team.
- The behaviours a leader must demonstrate to lead their team to their performance edge.

The behaviour of the leader is crucial

A leader has a special place in the team. As well as being a team member, they also have a helicopter view of the team and ultimately lead the team to success. How the leader behaves has a much greater impact on the team than any other team member's behaviour. Team members pay huge attention to what their leader does and how they 'show up' each day. Leaders need to understand this visibility and the impact their behaviour can have on the team. Being much more conscious of your impact as a leader (and possible interference – more on this in Chapter 8) in the team is essential to creating a high-performing team.

Through our research on hundreds of teams, we've identified several specific behaviours that leaders need to embrace to enable the conditions for success in a high-performing

148 Leading Edge

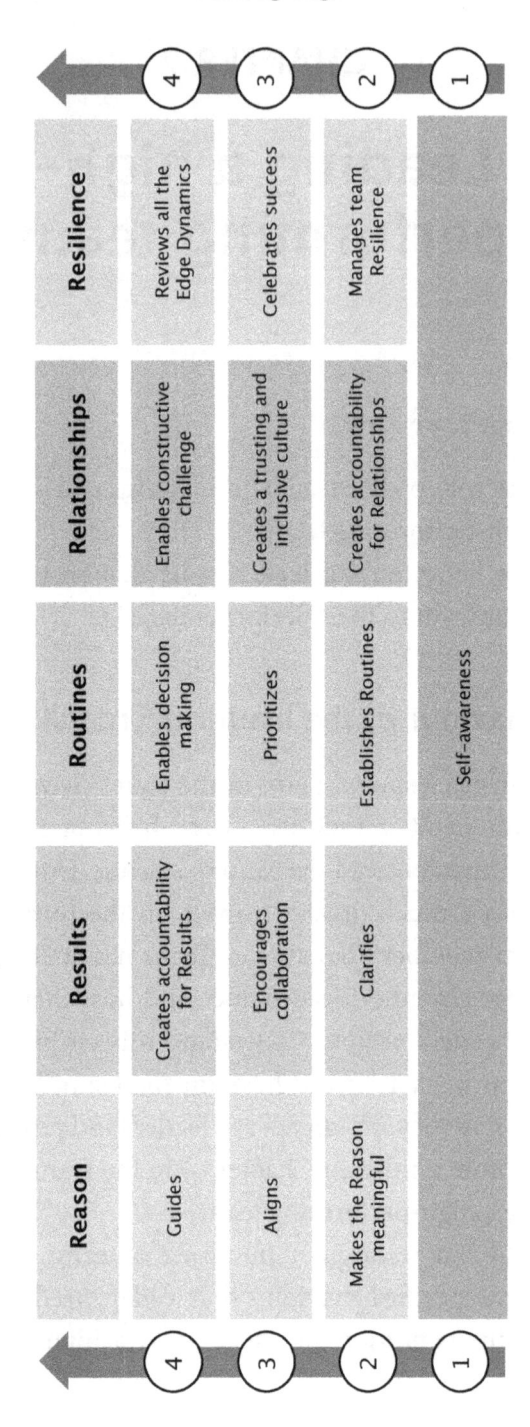

Reason	Results	Routines	Relationships	Resilience
Guides	Creates accountability for Results	Enables decision making	Enables constructive challenge	Reviews all the Edge Dynamics
Aligns	Encourages collaboration	Prioritizes	Creates a trusting and inclusive culture	Celebrates success
Makes the Reason meaningful	Clarifies	Establishes Routines	Creates accountability for Relationships	Manages team Resilience

Self-awareness

team. Start with self-awareness, then build your skills from the bottom of the diagram, working your way up.

Self-awareness

One of the most important skills a leader can have, and the differentiating skill that will set one leader apart from the rest, is self-awareness. This is the ability to see and know your own strengths and weaknesses, the things that trigger and motivate you and how you impact others. There's not one style for all situations and all people, so you need to be able to adjust your behaviour to suit different situations and people. If you're not aware of yourself in relation to others and the impact you have on your team members in particular, you'll miss critical things and that impact will be undermined. Sometimes people think that they're self-aware, but actually are only looking at things from the viewpoint of themselves. Real self-awareness is multi-dimensional. In fact, we would summarize self-awareness in three dimensions.

Awareness of self

This is being aware of your own strengths, weaknesses and motivations. You can gain awareness of this via a range of tools, including a quick self-assessment (see page 160), a personality assessment or by asking for feedback from your team members.

Awareness of self and others

This is being aware of your own strengths, weaknesses and motivations and how they impact other people, positively and negatively. It's being a fly on the wall in your own conversations with others and noticing what you're doing and saying and how the other person reacts. Or it's writing an email and imagining the impact it might have on the other person or observing their response to that email. It's noticing how your behaviour can change with different people.

Awareness of self and others in different contexts

This is being aware of how you impact other people, positively and negatively, and differently in different contexts. It's realizing that a strength with one person in one context will be positively impactful and in a different context with the same person will be negatively impactful. It's using that knowledge to shift and flex your behaviour according to the context and the person. It's noticing that you behave differently in different contexts with different people and using that difference in a positive way.

> **Team case study**
> One leader we worked with had massive ambition for her team, wanting them to achieve and sustain high performance. They were all very capable, intelligent, hard-working individuals but the team wasn't cohesive in any way. The biggest issue the leader would complain about was a lack of accountability in the team. Without accountability, no team will ever achieve high performance as the responsibility will sit firmly on the leader's shoulders alone. The leader lacked the self-awareness to realize that she was,

> for a great part, creating that lack of accountability. She'd micromanage the team, getting involved in decision-making and details that the team members could do on their own without her. She was getting in the way of her team on a daily basis, so it was no surprise that they weren't being accountable for the team's outcomes. The message her behaviour was sending was, 'I'm responsible for these outcomes so I'm going to step in and make sure they happen.' We worked with the team to identify where the accountability could be shifted from the leader to everyone in the team. We also worked with the leader to let go and reinforce that in her day-to-day interactions with the team. Two months later, the team is in a very different place, with full accountability for the team's Results and other Edge Dynamics.

Ultimately, it's great to be self-aware but that self-awareness means nothing if you don't do anything with it. True self-awareness goes further than just knowing something about yourself, it's using that knowledge to have a greater positive impact on your team. This is one of the keys to high performance in teams. It's very unlikely, probably impossible, to achieve high performance without a self-aware leader. Leaders with great self-awareness also help others to develop the skill of self-awareness themselves. They'll give feedback and coach their team members to raise their self-awareness. They'll build a culture of feedback within the team that promotes trust, constructive conflict and openness.

'Take your ego out of the game. Being a leader is about the people in your team, not yourself.'

Paul Howland
NATO Communications and
Information Agency, Chief C2

As well as self-awareness, the Edge Dynamics of Reason (Chapter 2), Results (Chapter 3), Routines (Chapter 4), Relationships (Chapter 5) and Resilience (Chapter 6) are all essential to develop and sustain high performance. We've identified the critical behaviours leaders need to unleash each of these Edge Dynamics.

Reason

As leader, you play a crucial role in creating clarity of Reason for the team. You do this through the following behaviours.

Makes the Reason meaningful

The leader of a high-performing team ensures that the team's Reason inspires and energizes the team. They help team members to identify their team Reason and what makes it meaningful to them both as individuals and as a team. They ensure that the team Reason is BMI (brief, memorable and inspirational) and they can articulate it to each other and people outside the team easily. The team Reason needs to add value to the team beyond just delivery of tasks. It needs to connect with team members at the emotional level.

Aligns

The leader of a high-performing team aligns team members and the team to the team Reason in the context of organizational needs. The leader helps the team to see their place in the organization and how they're contributing to the organization's success. They also help individuals in the team to share their own reasons for being in the team and to connect team members to each other. The leader also helps the team to adjust the team Reason as the context the team is working in shifts.

Guides

The leader of a high-performing team guides the team to focus on the team Reason. They continually focus the team's attention on the Reason, particularly in times of challenge or crisis. They know that the Reason is what holds the team together and use the Reason to provide 'glue' for the team. They find opportunities to keep talking about the team's Reason regularly and connect it to everything that the team is doing. They use it to support decision-making and encourage team members to do so also.

Results

The following behaviours will enable your team to deliver exceptional Results.

Clarifies

The leader of a high-performing team consistently strives to create clarity for the team. They know that a powerful gift they can give to their team is clarity – of objectives, accountabilities and expectations. They know that clarity isn't just a one-time thing, so they continuously strive to review clarity in the team. They challenge assumptions – both their own and those of team members. They're curious about what people are doing and constantly facilitate discussions in the team about it. They help the team to prioritize by regularly clarifying what the team is accountable for delivering. They keep things simple for the team (they know that less is more when it comes to Results) and they help the team to focus on the things that will make the biggest difference. They always keep the team's accountabilities and their progress towards them visible. They review team accountabilities regularly and adjust them when needed.

Encourages collaboration

The leader of a high-performing team facilitates and encourages collaboration between team members to achieve team accountabilities. They move beyond a focus on individual performance and actively encourage team members to work together to get things done. They regularly talk about collaboration in the team and ask questions of team members about how they're collaborating with others in the team. They understand the power of collaboration for solving complex problems and actively build interdependence within their team to harness this. They're also aware of over-collaboration and they work with their team members to avoid it and manage it when it arises. They use collaborative opportunities within the team for stretch and growth.

Creates accountability for Results

The leader of a high-performing team holds the team and team members accountable for Results. They ensure that every team member has clear accountability for their own individual objectives and expectations. They also challenge the team to be collectively responsible for the whole team's accountabilities. They encourage a sense of ownership of what the team achieves together. They identify where there are shared accountabilities and actively promote them within the team.

Routines

The following leader behaviours will help your team to create effective Routines that support high performance.

Establishes Routines

The leader of a high-performing team helps the team to establish good, solid Routines that add value. They have a continuous improvement mindset. They facilitate discussions about the team's Routines and challenge the team to adapt them to current contexts and needs. They continuously ask, 'Is this a good use of our time?' and encourage team members to do the same. They're aware of the impacts between Routines and other Edge Dynamics and design their Routines with care to support those other Edge Dynamics. They look beyond just achievement of a task to consider what Routines will take the team to high performance in the most effective way. They're conscious about which team member needs to be involved in various Routines, with one eye on inclusion and the other on efficiency. They're able to articulate why certain team members are involved so that no one feels excluded.

Prioritizes

The leader of a high-performing team assists the team to prioritize action. The leader is aware of workloads in the team and knows that there will always be more work than anyone can ever do. They know that their role is to prioritize work for the team and manage the team's stakeholders appropriately to ensure that they're focusing on the greatest value tasks. They observe their team and know when workloads are high. They create Routines to help the team to prioritize and increase effectiveness.

Enables decision-making

The leader of a high-performing team enables the team to make decisions without them. They have a process for making decisions in different contexts and topics. They have criteria that help with making decisions. They understand that decision-making needs a different process depending on the level of risk and the context in which the team is working (e.g. crisis or business as usual). They ensure that the team is aware of decision-making processes in the team and that decisions are made at the right level. They make sure that processes are discussed with the team, agreed with them and adjusted when needed. They have a process for keeping team members informed of decisions that are made by others. They support decisions that are made by team members without them.

Relationships

As leader, you play an important role in the Relationships within your team – both your Relationship with each team member and their Relationships with each other. Demonstrate these behaviours to maximize the Relationships in your team.

Creates accountability for Relationships

The leader of a high-performing team holds the team accountable for demonstrating agreed behaviours. They start by ensuring that the team has a set of agreed behaviours that they all commit to following. They then actively role-model those behaviours themselves and give team members feedback on the behaviours within the team. They positively reinforce and recognize when team members are demonstrating the agreed behaviours. They also challenge individuals who don't follow the agreed behaviours and hold them personally accountable for their behaviour in the team. They encourage team members to hold each other accountable for those behaviours.

Creates a trusting and inclusive culture

The leader of a high-performing team creates a culture of trust and inclusion within the team. They know that trust is essential for a high-performing team and actively seek high levels of trust in their team. They know that trust is built by continuous small actions every day and not a one-off event. They consider how their Routines build trust in this way. They also know that inclusion is critical for good decision-making, problem-solving and Resilience. They care authentically about their team and enable team members to care about each other.

Enables constructive challenge

The leader of a high-performing team expects and facilitates constructive challenge and diverse perspectives in the team. They understand the value of constructive challenge in teams and that it enables better decision-making and commitment to those decisions. They know that it facilitates the team's growth as it enables a broader view of their challenges and develops their thinking skills. They create Routines that provide opportunities to develop constructive challenge in the team. The leader invites constructive challenge into team conversations.

Resilience

To maintain high performance and Resilience in your team, the following leader behaviours are essential.

Manages team Resilience

The leader of a high-performing team actively manages the energy and workload of team members. They set an appropriate, sustainable but challenging pace for the team and adjust it according to the context the team is working in. They notice peaks in workload and encourage breaks to help the team recharge. They create opportunities for team members to substitute for each other enabling breaks to be impactful for the team. They know that a benefit of this is that others in the team grow and develop. They help team members to manage their energy levels throughout the day to ensure maximum productivity and engagement.

Celebrates success

The leader of a high-performing team ensures that the team regularly celebrates team successes. They monitor progress against the team's Reason and Results and recognize the whole team when they achieve a milestone. They celebrate successful fulfilment of the team's Edge Dynamics, focusing on both the *what* and the *how*. They celebrate individual contribution to team achievements as well as what the whole team achieves. They celebrate small wins regularly and pay sufficient attention to the big wins when they happen. They involve the team in deciding how to celebrate.

Reviews all the Edge Dynamics

The leader of a high-performing team constantly reviews, adjusts and refreshes all the Edge Dynamics to anticipate change for the team. They have a continuous eye on what's going on in and around the team that could necessitate change within the team. They have Routines for scanning the team's horizon and noticing what might affect them. They know that every time a team member joins or leaves, the team becomes a new team again. The dynamics within that team have changed, so everything needs to be reviewed and refreshed accordingly. This is the essence of being agile and is fundamental for sustaining high performance. The leader knows that this is where high-performing teams get stuck and lose their ability to perform at the highest levels. They encourage the team to continuously learn from everything – their successes and their failures – to enable future improvements.

To help you think about where to start with these behaviours, we've created a self-assessment of the foundation level leader behaviours below. Think about each leader behaviour and score it on the following scale:

1 – Totally disagree
2 – Somewhat disagree
3 – Neither agree nor disagree
4 – Somewhat agree
5 – Totally agree

Leader behaviour	Score
I'm aware of my own strengths, weaknesses and motivations	
I'm aware of how my strengths, weaknesses and motivations impact other people, positively and negatively	
I'm aware of how my strengths, weaknesses and motivations impact other people, positively and negatively, even in different contexts	
I make sure that my team's Reason inspires and energizes my team	
I consistently strive to create clarity for my team about team accountabilities	
I facilitate and encourage collaboration between team members to achieve team accountabilities	
I hold the team accountable for demonstrating agreed behaviours	
I help the team establish good, solid Routines that add value	
I actively manage the energy and workload of team members	
Total score	

When you've scored all the questions, add up the total and enter it into the last row.

Interpreting your score:

- 36–45: You have great foundational leader behaviours. Consider extending your awareness to the next level behaviours for each Edge Dynamic.
- 27–35: Your leader behaviours are developing and could still do with some work. Consider which behaviours you'd like to develop further.
- 9–34: Your leader behaviours could do with considerable work. Choose two or three behaviours to focus on to develop first.

Consider the following coaching questions to help you with this:

- Which leader behaviours will you prioritize to develop further?
- What action will you take to develop these leader behaviours?

Leading a high-performing team – a summary

Through our research on hundreds of teams, we've identified several specific behaviours that leaders need to embrace to enable the conditions for success in a high-performing team.

Self-awareness

This is the ability to see and know your own strengths and weaknesses, the things that trigger and motivate you and how you impact others. This is an over-arching behaviour that leaders of high-performing teams need.

Reason

- Makes the Reason meaningful
- Aligns
- Guides

Results

- Clarifies
- Encourages collaboration
- Creates accountability for Results

Routines

- Establishes Routines
- Prioritizes
- Enables decision-making

Relationships

- Creates accountability for Relationships
- Creates a trusting and inclusive culture
- Expects constructive challenge

Resilience

- Manages team Resilience
- Celebrates success
- Reviews all the Edge Dynamics

CHAPTER 8

Accelerators and interferences

In this chapter, we explore:

- How to speed up the performance of your team (accelerators).
- What gets in the way of the performance of your team (interferences).

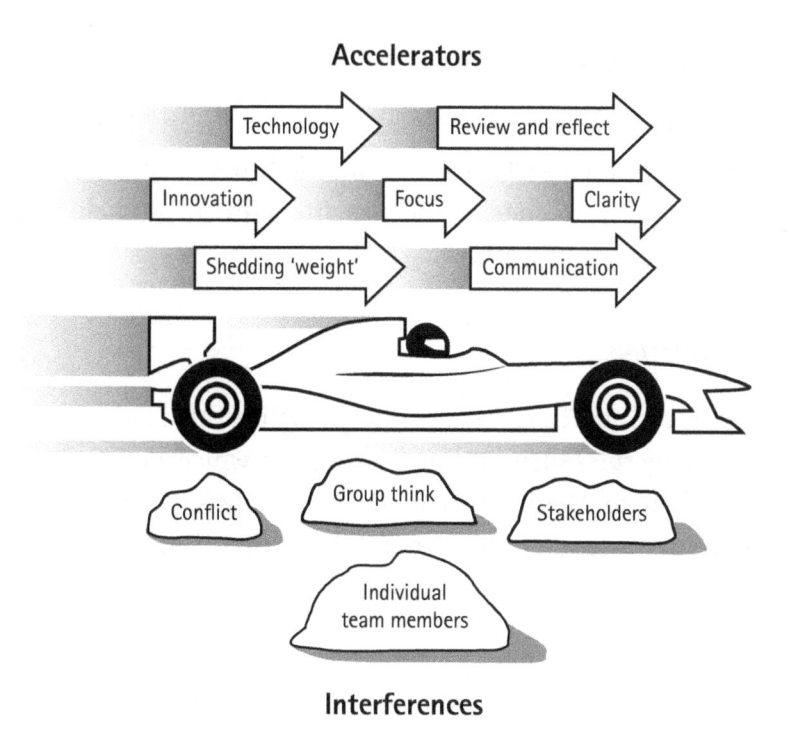

Accelerators

Technology
Review and reflect
Innovation
Focus
Clarity
Shedding 'weight'
Communication

Conflict
Group think
Stakeholders
Individual team members

Interferences

Think like a Formula 1 team

Every team can identify the factors that will maximize or get in the way of high performance. We call these the accelerators and the interferences. Many of the teams we start working with are good teams. The reason that they're not high-performing is often because they're not utilizing their accelerators effectively and not minimizing their interferences. Many of them haven't even noticed them! Once you know what they are, it's like identifying your team's superpowers and kryptonite. We like to use the analogy of the sport of Formula 1 (F1). This sport is all about speed, high performance and it's a very much a team sport. In fact, one team in F1 extends to hundreds of people in every race, all focused on one objective – to win.

Accelerators

Here are a few examples of the accelerators for an F1 team. At the end of each section, we've included some questions that will help you to consider how their context might help you think about your team.

Innovation

The car in an F1 team is essential to high performance. There are many rules surrounding the car itself, which a team needs to adhere to. Despite this, there's plenty of space for innovation in the design of the car and the engine. This means that the car itself can be a competitive advantage if designed well and innovation in car/engine design can be a massive accelerator of performance. An example of this is the introduction of the halo in 2018 – a driver crash-protection system, which consists of a curved bar placed to protect the driver's head. A safer car not only protects the driver from harm, but it also enables the driver to feel safe enough to push the car harder and take a risk that they might not have done otherwise. This innovation has been key to success for many teams.

Moving away from F1 for a moment, in recent years, many teams have been forced to work from home, so have had to innovate the way that they work to be successful. Many teams used innovations in technology to ensure that they were still able to communicate and connect with each other. For example, one team that we worked with used a virtual whiteboard to share their task lists with each other, which meant that any team member could see what another team member was working on in a highly visual, adaptable way – a little innovation that made a big difference to the team. What innovation would make a big difference to your team? How do you ensure that the conditions for innovation are right within the team?

Technology

Technology is another example of an accelerator for F1 teams, who use a myriad of technology to measure, control, analyse and simulate every aspect of the car and engine. This enables them to adjust things in real time, prepare for pit stops and informs race and longer-term strategy. Without keeping their computing power at the bleeding edge, their performance would be hindered – eventually their technology would be so outdated that it would be obsolete and the team would no longer be able to compete.

How does technology accelerate the performance of your team? Is it fit for purpose? Are you continuously investing in the latest technology to keep your team at the leading edge?

Shedding 'weight'

The weight of the car is an obsession for F1 teams. 'Engineers estimate that a car can go 0.3 seconds per lap faster for every 10 kilograms of weight that's taken off the car. While this might not sound like a lot at first, in the context of Formula 1, three-tenths of a second can mean the difference between winning and coming second.'[22] It's a huge challenge to make a car lighter, as everything that's on the car is perceived to be essential – they've already been designed to have as little weight as possible, and yet there's always something that can be made lighter or removed.

Every team we work with has the same challenge. There's always too much work, not enough resources and not enough time. Everything is perceived to be essential and nothing is ever removed. How can you help your team to shed 'weight' by prioritizing tasks and reclarifying what's most important? It can be helpful here to think about the 80/20 rule (mentioned in Chapter 3). What are the 20% of tasks that deliver 80% of the value to your team? What can your team remove? How can you help them to say 'no' elegantly?

---

[22] https://flowracers.com/blog/why-are-f1-drivers-weighed/

Focus

An F1 team has a singular focus – to win championships. This clarity of Results is a huge accelerator for the team. It means that everything they do is in service of that objective. They create milestones to be achieved to deliver against this. It's about winning the qualifier, then the fastest lap, then the race itself, then the championship.

To what extent is clarity of Results with associated milestones an accelerator for your team? How can you help maintain your team's focus on those Results? How do you help them to break their Results down into manageable chunks via a roadmap? How do you help them to maintain focus even when they miss a milestone? How do you celebrate achieving a milestone as a team?

Clarity of roles and responsibilities

More than 20 people make up the F1 pit crew. They're responsible for stabilizing the car, changing the tyres, making adjustments to the aerodynamics and safely releasing the car, all in under two seconds – if everything goes well.

Everyone in the pit knows exactly what their role is as there's no room for confusion – this could be costly in terms of both time and safety. Each member of the pit stop team will practise until their role becomes muscle memory and they don't need to think about it any more. They talk about not being able to remember the perfect pit stop, which suggests that they're in 'flow' in these moments, where they lose all sense of time and are just immersed in the task.

What about your team? Your team may not need to work in exactly the same way as an F1 pit stop team, but there are still parallels to be made. How clear are roles and responsibilities in your team? How often are your team able to get into a 'flow' state? How much does your team prepare for critical moments? How well do they understand the interdependencies between people in the team? How much accountability does each team member take for their role in the team and their contribution to the team's overall performance?

Communication

Communication is essential in an F1 team, particularly during a race, when they'll mostly communicate via radio. The team that doesn't communicate well, doesn't win. The F1 garage is a noisy place and it can be very hard to concentrate with all the bustle and activity going on around everyone. Team members wear headsets to cut the noise out and enable them to focus on what they need to hear, but what they're listening to varies from person to person. Different channels are set up to enable different groups to listen to their area of focus. A race engineer and the mechanics might be on one channel and the senior staff might be discussing race strategy on another. There are also general channels that all the team can listen in to and some channels are public to the other teams in the race. Very few people are hearing all the conversations, everyone is just hearing the things they need to complete their role with the minimum distraction.[23] F1 teams are very clear about which communication channels each person needs access to. Team members are conscious of minimizing distractions and maximizing focus by maintaining targeted, clear communications with the right people.

---

[23] www.redbullracing.com/int-en/bulls-guide-to-team-radio

From our experience, communication in many teams is poor. There's often either one of two extremes – too much communication or too little. Very few teams spend the time to get really targeted, focused, clear communication Routines in place. When thinking about communication in your team, what enables them to be sufficiently informed, while at the same time focusing without distraction at critical moments? What Routines will help with this (see Chapter 4)? Who really needs to be involved in which conversations? When do you need consensus and when can the team or individual make the decision?

Review and reflect

Whether a Grand Prix has gone well or not, there's always plenty for F1 teams to review and reflect on in the team afterwards. The team always has their eye on the next race and to achieve this they need to analyse and review the previous one. They'll highlight and praise the positives as well as examining what went wrong and could be improved for next time. There's a detailed review process after every race, often culminating in a full team meeting, which could involve up to 500 people.

How often does your team review and reflect to improve how you do things? What Routines do you have for continuous improvement? What Routines do you have for learning from each other and for feedback about how the team is doing?

Interferences

Here are a few example of the interferences for an F1 team. At the end of each section, we've included some questions that will help you to consider how their context might assist you in thinking about your team.

Conflict

Conflict (see Chapter 5) occurs in any team and can be a massive interference to high performance. In F1, the most obvious conflict can occur between two drivers in the same team. Rivalries and favouritism can sometimes create catastrophic outcomes for the team – for example, when two drivers on the same team collide with each other, causing the team to be out of the race completely. Conflict like this means that team members are no longer working towards the team's objectives. They're more focused on their own personal objective of winning. Another issue could be a lack of conflict, when team members are afraid to speak up about issues within the team. This can lead to poor decision-making, a lack of accountability and unspoken frustrations. It can also undermine race reviews.

Both conflict and an absence of conflict are a challenge for a team. What's happening in your team? Are they in conflict to the point of mutual destruction or are they not speaking up at all? How can you help your team members to overcome their differences and focus on the team objectives before their own personal objectives? How can you help team members to speak up and challenge each other respectfully and constructively in service of better outcomes?

Individual team members

Sometimes a driver has to leave an F1 team because their personal agenda isn't aligned with that of the team. This causes them to be out of synch and, at worst, in direct opposition to the goals of the team. This leads to underperformance, conflict and dysfunction.

We see this happening in organizational teams too. Sometimes a team member doesn't align with the goals of the team or other team members. They can become disruptive and toxic to the climate within the team. The rest of the team might feel like they can't rely on that person to get things done. We all know when we're in this situation. Team meetings can feel painful and the rest of the team really feels it. Sometimes feedback and coaching can help them to realign with the team and sometimes the best solution for everyone is for the individual to leave the team.

Do you have team members in your team who are misaligned or disruptive? Someone who's not performing as expected? How can you manage this? How can you coach them and give them feedback on the impact they're having on the team? How can you help them to get aligned? Or, as a last resort, how can you help them to leave the team?

Group think

When problems occur in an F1 team, it's important that they're identified and resolved quickly. Ensuring that there's a breadth of perspectives and really challenging assumptions is critical to continuously improving performance. If people just accept a response as 'the answer' automatically, without critically analysing that response, there's a danger of making poor decisions and not getting to the root cause. This is what we call 'group think'. This is when the desire for group consensus overrides people's common-sense desire to present alternatives, critique a position or express an unpopular opinion.

Team members aren't even aware of the underlying assumptions the team is making and are unwittingly narrowing their perspective as a result.

How often does your team succumb to 'group think'? What's the impact of this? How can you get them to think more critically and challenge their own assumptions more regularly? What Routines can help with this?

Other teams/stakeholders

In F1 we hear a lot in the media about tensions between teams, drivers and the sport's governing body, the FIA (Fédération Internationale de l'Automobile). This conflict and the interactions between the sport's various stakeholders makes for good news stories; however, it can also impede high performance. A team is never an island. They're part of a broader system with parts that they interact with, compete with, support and rely on. Paying attention to the whole system and understanding the consequences of changes to it is essential. Where there's an interdependence between teams in the system, your team must be in alignment with them. Competing agendas can affect the team negatively. Your team will need to be proactive in managing the Relationships you have with these key stakeholders. You'll need to notice and influence shifts in those Relationships as they occur.

Which teams and stakeholders are the most important for your team? What are Relationships like with these groups? How aligned are your goals with theirs? What Routines do you have for reviewing, improving and maintaining alignment in the Relationships you have with key stakeholders?

> **Team case study**
>
> This team had a key, interdependent Relationship with another team. Everything was going smoothly until the leader of the other team changed. Suddenly, the other team's priorities, vision and strategy changed and it was now misaligned with our client team. This had a massive impact on the client team's ability to perform. It wasn't until they re-engaged with the other team to create alignment, review vision and strategy and create a new way of working together that both teams were able to perform to their potential again.

Accelerators and interferences are dynamic

We've named a few examples here of both accelerators and interferences and each team is unique and will have their own. Work with your team to identify which are the most important for you, so that you can maximize the potential of your team. They may also shift and change over time, so create a Routine to check in every now and then. Working on one may also affect the others. They're often interconnected. Working on alignment, for example, builds clarity of roles and responsibilities. The aim is never to eliminate the interferences completely (that's an impossible task) but to strive to minimize and pre-empt them. See them as an opportunity to create continuous improvement and to challenge your team to innovate how they do things.

Are you an interference or an accelerator?

All leaders like to think that they only accelerate the performance of their team and that they add value all the time. One of the toughest realizations any leader can have is that they can get in the way of their own team, negatively impacting performance and being an interference. We see this all the time. Increasing your self-awareness and strengthening your behaviours as a leader (see Chapter 7) will support you in ensuring that you're an accelerator more than you're an interference.

Here are some examples of interference by a leader.

Micromanaging

This is a classic interference that usually comes from a place of positive intention. The leader sees themselves as helping the team and speeding things up when actually they're having the opposite effect – they're disempowering and slowing down the team. Micromanaging means that the leader is acting at an inappropriate level in the team. They're operating at one level (or more) below where they should be and hindering their own ability to see the bigger picture for the team. When a leader micromanages a team, they often complain of being overloaded, with a team that doesn't take accountability for outcomes.

Decision-making bottleneck

We often see teams where the leader makes all the decisions themselves, even really minor ones. The team doesn't feel empowered to make decisions without involving the leader. This becomes a problem for the team as the leader becomes the bottleneck and may slow decision-making down for the team.

Tolerating poor performance

One of the things that team members notice acutely is when poor performance by individuals in the team isn't dealt with appropriately. Either it's addressed half-heartedly, or it's ignored by the leader. One leader we worked with hadn't even noticed there was an issue with poor performance in his team. It was causing great frustration and disengagement in the rest of the team. The leader thought he had given the team member feedback about their poor performance, yet it continued. When it was discussed with the team member, they thought they were doing just fine! It's important to address poor performance head-on.

Lack of accountability

Many leaders complain about their team members not demonstrating accountability for the team's objectives. They feel like that accountability sits solely on their shoulders, team members only focus on their own individual objectives and take little notice of the team as a whole. Team members see that as the leader's role exclusively. We also find that leaders themselves are enabling this behaviour unwittingly. They don't hold their team accountable for team outcomes, they measure success through individual objectives. They don't demand collaboration between team members and they fill the gap themselves when it comes to team objectives.

These are just a few examples of ways in which leaders might interfere with the performance of their team. To what extent do these apply to you? What would your team say about this? How would they perceive that you get in the way of their performance? To find out, you could run a session with them to discuss the accelerators and interferences in the team and how to maximize / minimize them. Ask them to give you feedback personally about how you're an accelerator or an interference. Make it safe for them to do so and consider helping them to do this in an anonymous way if you don't think they're able to tell you in person.

Take a look at the 'Escalation Analysis' tool on our website to determine what your team is regularly escalating to you for resolution.[24] This can give you an insight as to what kinds of things might be hindering the team and your role in overcoming them.

Accelerators and interferences – a summary

Every team can identify the factors that will maximize or get in the way of high performance. We call these the accelerators and the interferences.

Examples of accelerators

- Innovation
- Technology

---

[24] www.management-dynamics.com/leading-edge

- Shedding 'weight'
- Focus
- Clarity of roles and responsibilities
- Communication
- Review and reflect

Examples of interferences

- Conflict
- Individual team members
- Group think
- Other teams/stakeholders

Work with your team to identify which are the most important accelerators and interferences, so that you can maximize the potential of your team. They may also shift and change over time, so create a Routine to check in every now and then.

Consider in what way you as leader are an interference and an accelerator for your team.

Some examples of interference by leaders are:

- Micromanaging
- Decision-making bottlenecks
- Tolerating poor performance
- Lack of accountability

Work to maximize the way in which you can be an accelerator for your team and minimize the interferences.

CHAPTER 9

Team composition for high performance

In this chapter, we explore:

- The different types of team and how to develop them to high performance.
- The different contexts teams work in and some of the impacts this can have on high performance.
- How diversity and inclusion in teams affects performance.

Types of teams

In our experience of working with hundreds of teams, we've observed that there are two types of team – simple and complex. Neither type is right or wrong, better or worse, it's just useful to know what type of team you have so that you can invest your time wisely in developing them to high performance. Each has their own unique set of needs and require a different approach to applying the Edge Dynamics.

Simple teams

We define a simple team as one where all the team members have the same leader but very little, if any, interdependence between each other to get their jobs done. They can deliver their role independently of their colleagues within the team. They may have interdependencies outside the team and they may do a similar role to others in the team.

Sales teams are often simple teams as they're made up of a group of salespeople all doing similar roles, maybe with different territories/accounts/verticals. Their main interface in the team is with the leader. Each of them will have Relationships and interdependencies outside the team, such as the product manager, the customer service team or the logistics team, but have few interdependencies within the team itself. The problem with a simple team like this is that it can be hard to create a feeling of 'team' and belonging and, as a result, turnover can be high.

The Edge Dynamics are still just as relevant in a simple team. Applying them is usually easier as they're more straightforward to establish and require less effort and discussion to create. A simple team still needs a clear, compelling Reason and individuals need to be able to connect with it. That's usually enough, you don't need to labour the point or go deeply into a detailed process to create the team Reason. They also need clarity of team Results and their own individual accountabilities. In relation to the team Results, they need to understand what they should be collaborating on (e.g. sharing best practice, streamlining processes, etc.) and what they shouldn't. They need simple, effective, low-effort Routines. They need good solid Relationships that create a sense of community and belonging. Finally, they need sufficient levels of Resilience to manage team members' energy levels and withstand setbacks to the team.

Forcing a simple team to collaborate for the sake of collaboration is a waste of time and resources, yet we see it happening all the time. Leaders invest huge amounts of time in team-building without really understanding the type of team that they have and where the greatest value is. There have to be benefits to the individuals concerned as well as to the team as a whole. Simple teams, in our experience, collaborate well on sharing best practice or innovation and continuous improvement projects. They'll need to be given permission to collaborate and be rewarded for doing so.

If you have a simple team, the key is to establish a compelling Reason (Chapter 2) and clear team Results (Chapter 3) that give team members an incentive to collaborate and connect with each other. Develop simple and effective Routines (Chapter 4) that build good Relationships (Chapter 5). In a simple team, Resilience (Chapter 6) is a great foundation for team collaboration as team members learn to substitute for each other as needed.

Complex teams

We define a complex team as one where there are multiple interdependencies among team members, who rely on others in the team to get things done.

The benefit of a complex team is that you can complete complicated tasks much more effectively and realize the advantages of working together with others to solve problems and improve how things are done. The ability to collaborate, explore different points of view and gain new perspectives enables a team to be innovative. In fact, research shows that a group of people will make a better decision than one person alone.[25]

---

[25] www.forbes.com/sites/eriklarson/2017/09/21/new-research-diversity-inclusion-better-decision-making-at-work/?sh=5142d8704cbf

Interdependence creates complexity because of the number of Relationships and touchpoints that are required to be successful between team members. We're talking about human beings here, and people are wonderfully different and complex in their own right. It's easy for misunderstandings and conflict to occur between people. It's also common for people to be misaligned as to how the work gets done without investing time in discussions and agreements. Therefore, a complex team needs more support in setting up the team for success. If you lead a complex team, you'll need to invest time and effort in building Relationships (Chapter 5) and Routines (Chapter 4) for interdependence. You'll need to ensure that the whole team is clear about the Reason (Chapter 2) and Results (Chapter 3) and keep reviewing them to maintain that clarity and Resilience (Chapter 6).

Complex teams are also complicated because they change constantly. New people join, people leave and the context in which they operate changes around them. This means that the team continuously needs to adapt and evolve to sustain high performance. Reviewing all the Edge Dynamics regularly is a critical Routine. A complex team is never 'done' when it comes to high performance.

A risk in a complex team is over-collaboration. It's easy to over-complicate processes and interdependencies. A few years ago, when our team was still quite new, we encouraged more collaboration among team members. The team jumped at this and enthusiastically started working together on projects. A month later, they were working on everything together, which, while initially was a nice experience for them, was also costly for us and also very inefficient and slow, which ultimately frustrated them. Collaboration needs to add value to everyone, while at the same time increasing productivity.

Leadership teams are always, by default, complex teams. However, not all leadership teams operate as if they're a complex team and may act as if they're a simple team instead. You can see how this might happen – a leadership team usually comprises heads of functions who have their own large functional teams below them in the organizational hierarchy. They may come together as a leadership team only once a month (or whatever rhythm the team has established), whereas they're operating with their functional teams on a daily basis. Their personal credibility is primarily about their functional area of responsibility. The organization rewards them for the success of their own function. The emphasis, therefore, quite naturally, is the team they lead rather than the leadership team they're part of. If this is happening at the leadership team level, you can guarantee that it's mirrored further down the organization.

We're often invited into a team to help break down the silos that this emphasis creates. In practice, these leadership teams lack a compelling team Reason, have low levels of accountability for team Results and strategic decisions that are made, have poor Relationships, boring and inefficient Routines and little Resilience. As complex teams, they should be capitalizing on the untapped potential to create true high performance. And as a leadership team, the benefits for the whole organization are massive. This is where the competitive edge will be realized.

What type of team do you have? What type of team would add the greatest value to the organization? If you have a simple team, how could you invest wisely in the team's development and cohesion to create a sense of belonging and collective purpose? If you have a complex team, are they operating as such? Many teams who should be complex teams and achieve so much more are designed and function as simple teams.

How can you enable your team to collaborate more effectively without the risk of over-collaboration?

Matrix teams

Many organizations that we work with have implemented matrix approaches. A matrix organization is a structure in which teams report to multiple leaders. They can be hugely beneficial to organizations as they break down silos, reduce duplication of effort, minimize cost and provide career development. However, they also create complexity because people effectively sit in two or more teams, which means that they have interdependency with multiple team members. Therefore, they need to develop and maintain Relationships with a much wider group of people than is needed in a traditional hierarchical structure. Let's explore some of the things you should consider if anyone in your team (or your whole team) is part of a matrix structure.

Competing priorities

When people report to multiple leaders, competing priorities can be one of the biggest challenges that can be created. Each leader has their own strategy, goals and accountabilities that they're driving in their team. These can sometimes be perceived as conflicting and the team member will need to use excellent influencing skills to manage both of their bosses to fulfil both desired outcomes successfully. Sometimes it's not possible to keep both parties happy and one will be achieved at the expense of the other.

> **Team case study**
>
> This is a health and safety team for an organization with several production sites. The team members are all part of two teams. Firstly, the health and safety team, which is all the health and safety specialists reporting into the health and safety director. Each of them is also part of a second team, the production site that they support, reporting to the site leader. The health and safety team has a strategy that they're working to achieve, mostly long-term initiatives and priorities focused on consistently improving health and safety practices across the business. The individual team members, who are based at their site, also manage daily health and safety incidents that occur at the site. The site leader naturally wants to address these issues and ensure that they don't happen again – an important and urgent task. This can take over from the health and safety team priorities, which are important but not urgent. The natural tension that occurs between these 'competing priorities' creates complexity for the team members to manage on a day-to-day basis.

Tactical vs strategic

Another issue that can occur in a matrix team, which the previous example also illustrates, is the tension between the tactical and the strategic. All teams feel this, but it can be particularly acute in a matrix structure. Usually, one team focuses more on the strategic, while the other has more of a tactical focus. Whenever this tension occurs, team members invariably move towards the tactical as it's often urgent, immediate and right in front of them. The task that needs to be done right now often demands their attention the most. In this environment, team members need to ensure that they have a Routine to enable them to be more critical of the urgent, tactical things that pop up and see where they're undermining the strategic priorities. They need to link tasks with the team Results and the team Reason. They need to learn to balance both appropriately and will need your support as their leader to help them do this. It's not an easy thing to do and you may need to have a Routine yourself (and sufficient Relationships) to work with the other leader(s) they report to so that you can resolve the conflict together.

Lack of belonging

When people are part of more than one team, they can feel like they belong either nowhere, or in just one of the teams. It's unusual for people to feel like they belong to both teams unless the leaders work hard to create this. People feel they belong the most where they understand the Reason and Results and have good Relationships with others in the team. Where they feel that they're contributing to team objectives and are valued. Where they're included in decision-making. Where they make regular connection with their fellow team members and can get to know each other as people. A sense of belonging creates loyalty, and when competing priorities pop up, invariably the team to which they feel the greatest belonging will take a natural precedence. As a leader of a matrixed team, therefore, it's important to help people feel that sense of belonging to your team and to develop Relationships within the team. You may need to work harder at it than if your team wasn't matrixed but the investment will be worth it.

When leading a matrix team, you'll need to focus on making sure all team members understand the team's Reason and its connection to their matrixed roles. They need to connect with the Reason personally and see how it benefits the other teams that they're part of too. They need clarity of Results in terms of expectations of them from all stakeholders in the organization. They need a Routine for gaining agreement when there are competing priorities and for how to resolve them, and a clear decision-making process. Team Routines must acknowledge the fact that they're part of multiple teams so have a lot of demands on their time. They need strong Relationships, both within your team and the other matrixed teams. They need to be able to keep people informed and appropriately involved, while at the same time being able to challenge team members constructively. Team members who are working in a matrix environment are the most likely to experience burnout as they're operating in an extremely complex context. As a leader it's particularly important to pay attention to their Resilience and how the dynamics in the team are affecting them.

Project teams

Project teams come in all sizes, from the small group of four or five people brought together to implement an improvement to a service, to a transformation team implementing a new system, with hundreds of people involved. Project teams also exist for varying lengths of time, from weeks to years. The larger the team, the more challenging the dynamics within it. Project teams are usually complex because there's interdependency built into the design of the team. They're also invariably a matrix structure. Project teams are also frequently much more dynamic than normal teams as people come and go for various stages of the project. For example, a coder won't be involved in the early stages of a system implementation when the project is being defined and scoped. They're only brought on board once the technical specification is agreed.

As a leader of a project team, you'll need to bear all of this in mind and be ready to create a strong kick-off for the team, where you'll define the team's Reason and Results and start to establish sufficient levels of Relationships in the team. If your team is large, focus on establishing Relationships at the sub-group level and set up Routines to help manage them appropriately. Then you'll need to manage the Resilience of your team and the peaks and troughs of workload. You'll also need to focus on the impacts on Relationships and other Edge Dynamics of people joining and leaving the team at various stages. You'll need to refresh the Reason, Results and Routines regularly to ensure that they're fit for purpose according to the stage of the project.

Team size

As with many things in life, when it comes to a team, size does matter. The optimal size of a team will depend on whether it's simple or complex. Simple teams can be much larger and still be effective. The main impact here of a large team is your capacity as a leader to manage all of your team members independently. We regularly see simple teams of 20–25 people. Ensure that you have great Routines for managing each team member individually. Don't waste team time talking about individual work. Instead, focus on sharing best practice, improving processes and looking at trends.

> 'You can't help 200 people directly, but the message spreads that the boss knows what is going on and takes care of you.'
>
> **Paul Howland**
> **NATO Communications and Information Agency**
> **Chief C2**

Team case study

A sales team that we worked with had a regular Monday morning meeting that lasted two hours. The agenda was effectively each team member giving an update on their focus for the week ahead. This was useful for the leader, as they gained an understanding of what each team member was doing, but completely irrelevant for everyone else. Each team member (apart from the leader) hated the meeting and spent most of the time catching up on their emails while the meeting took place. This was a waste of time and eroded team cohesion, preventing any form of collaboration. There were numerous ways of updating the team on planned work in a different way, such as everyone sending an instant message to the group first thing on a Monday morning with their update, or each person meeting with the leader individually and updating them that way.

Complex teams need to be much smaller – but not too small – to enable team members to effectively manage all the Relationships they need. Here, collaboration is key, but it takes time and, if too many people are involved, you risk over-collaboration and inefficiency. According to McKinsey, a leadership team comprising fewer than six people 'is likely to result in poorer decisions because of a lack of diversity, and slower decision-making because of a lack of bandwidth. Research also suggests that the team's effectiveness starts to diminish if there are more than ten people on it. Sub-teams start to form, encouraging divisive behaviour.'[26]

As we've discussed already, a high-performing team is one where everyone feels included in team meetings, decision-making and delivering the team's Results. The bigger the team, the harder it becomes to ensure that everyone is heard and included. Inclusive meetings will take longer when you have more people. If you have an hour-long meeting and everyone contributes to the meeting equally, in a team of six that's ten minutes each, in a team of ten that's six minutes each, and in a team of 15, it's only four minutes each. It's challenging to debate and discuss issues in an inclusive manner when you only have four minutes each! It then becomes essential as a leader for you to learn strong facilitation techniques, which will help speed up decision-making without undermining the quality of the conversation and the sharing of ideas and thoughts.

The bigger the team, the easier it is for cliques or sub-groups to form. Human beings naturally form groups,

---

[26] www.mckinsey.com/business-functions/people-and-organizational-performance/our-insights/high-performing-teams-a-timeless-leadership-topic

even within a team, and they'll happen along the lines of who has common interests, backgrounds and experiences. Cliques are, by their nature, excluding and should be avoided if you want a high-performing team. Challenge your team to spend time and build Relationships with people they have less in common with naturally. If cliques appear in your team, are you encouraging this in some way? Do you spend more time with some people in your team than with others? Be very careful of this as it will create a perception of favourites, which will hinder team cohesion and therefore performance.

Sometimes you'll have no choice about the size of the team that you lead – you need to work with what you've got. So how do you lead a large, complex team effectively so that they can be as high-performing as possible, despite their size? The most effective large, complex teams that we've worked with have focused on the following areas.

Decision-making

Decision-making in a large complex team can't be by consensus. You'll spend far too much time debating issues without ever really getting consensus. The highest-performing teams create sub-committees for key decisions and the debate and recommendations are delegated to that group. They bring their final recommendation to the whole team for final approval. For this to work, the whole team must trust their advice and recommendation, so the composition of the sub-committee is key, as is the process for final sign-off.

Interdependencies

In a large complex team, it's important not to set the expectation that everyone should collaborate with everyone in the team. This creates an impossible and very inefficient team that will be in meeting overload. Help your team to get clear on where the most impactful interdependencies lie and foster those Relationships. Everyone should have at least one interdependency in the team, but not too many.

Routines

Be very careful of your Routines in a large team. Maximize the chances of your team meetings being well attended by ensuring that they're value-added for everyone in the team (no boring updates) and that all discussions are relevant to at least two-thirds of the attendees. If the topic is relevant to any less than this, you'll need to set up a separate meeting of only the involved team members. Without this careful focus, Relationships, Results and Resilience will all be eroded quickly.

Virtual and hybrid teams

There are three team distribution types: co-located, virtual and hybrid teams.

Co-located teams

Traditionally, nearly all teams were co-located, when everyone was based in the same location and saw each other face to face pretty much every day. When teams are co-located, it's easier for people to build and maintain Relationships, to adjust Routines and to notice the Resilience levels within the team. This is only true if a team is all in the same physical space. The minute they're located in different buildings or on different floors of the same building, they're no longer a co-located team. We would say they're now a virtual team. If your team is co-located, you'll have an easier job of creating a real sense of belonging through the Relationships that team members will develop. Capitalize on the everyday opportunities the team will have to build trust and support each other. It's easier to use your physical environment (i.e. office walls and desks) to create visual reminders of the team Reason and progress against your team's Results. Co-located teams we've worked with have created posters with their team Reason on it. They display their team's Results scorecard on the wall. You'll also see benefits in your Routines as things like team 'stand-up' quick meetings and team shared lunches become so much easier than in the other team distribution types.

> **Team case study**
> We worked with one team who were based across two buildings next door to each other. The team had naturally split into two cliques or sub-teams by – you've guessed it – location. There was a strong 'them and us' culture and it was really affecting team performance. This was a constraint that the team needed to learn to deal with and put in place Routines to ensure collaboration across the two locations. For example, they took turns to work across the two buildings and had regular meetings and social events where people in the two buildings would come together face to face. This really started to erode the feeling of division and encouraged collaboration. They also identified 'Big

> Whats' (see Chapter 3), which required collaboration between team members and actively encouraged people to work together from different buildings. They set up regular face-to-face connects with each other to collaborate on their accountabilities.

Virtual teams

Virtual teams are teams where the team members are all in different locations – often spread around the world and across time zones. Sometimes virtual teams never meet each other face to face and rely on technology to communicate with each other. Technology can enable very strong Relationships to be established in virtual teams and no longer poses a barrier to performance. Having said this, it's more challenging to establish and maintain Relationships and a sense of belonging in a virtual team. More consistent effort is needed and it will require great Routines that enable frequent connection points for everyone in your team. You'll need to pay closer attention to the Resilience of your team and have Routines in place to help you and the team monitor this. Many virtual teams can be very creative about ways in which they can still have touchpoints for building Relationships and getting to know each other better.

It can be very easy to just focus on task in a virtual team. It can also be easy to set up very formulaic (read: 'boring') Routines in a virtual team, which won't engage people in the most effective way. Watch out for people multitasking during team meetings – this is a sure sign that they're bored. You may need to up the ante, increase the pace and level of interaction in the meetings. Don't be afraid to finish meetings early. You could also change the format and use all the wonderful opportunities that technology gives us, such as whiteboards, polling, music, video, etc, to add variety. Most importantly, ensure that every team member has their video on all the time when you're meeting, unless there's a very good (exceptional!) reason. It's almost impossible to build sufficient levels of trust with someone that you can't see.

Hybrid teams

Hybrid teams comprise a combination of co-located and virtual team members. This is the most common distribution of team now. Meetings may be a mix of people sitting in a room, with a few people dialling in from other locations. Sometimes it may be possible to get everyone together face to face, but these occurrences may only be infrequent. Routines become essential in this situation and you should consider how you use technology for the greatest impact. Design your meetings so that everyone gets involved and that those dialling in to a face-to-face meeting can hear what's going on and are included. We've seen many examples of meetings when the poor person dialling in to the meeting is completely forgotten about and effectively ignored! Sometimes it may be better to have everyone join the meeting virtually than to attempt a hybrid meeting, especially when the meeting room isn't set up well in terms of technology (e.g. video/audio).

Time zones can create several issues in your team, the most impactful being Resilience. When you have extended time zones covered in your team, it's important to pay attention to meeting times and how they affect a team member's working day. We work with several teams who span multiple time zones, from the USA to Europe, Asia and Australia, and it's easy for team Routines to revolve around the time zone represented the most in the team (or the time zone of the leader/head office). This means that the team members on the extremes of time difference are often disadvantaged and end up working either very early or very late in their day. This is usually not a problem if team meetings are infrequent, say a couple of times a year. But when they're weekly (or more) it can become exhausting. Very rarely do people feel they can flex their working days to allow for the additional hours, and the impact of tiredness on their ability to contribute at their best is apparent. These team members often end up feeling excluded and very much on the periphery as well as tired!

Cross-cultural teams

Most teams we work with have a mix of cultures within them, whether they're co-located, virtual or hybrid. It's rare to have a mono-cultural team and there are huge benefits to multi-cultural teams. It brings your team a wider variety of perspectives and experiences, which leads to better decision-making and innovation. Having said that, it also can bring challenges, particularly in Relationships, as people tend to like (and therefore trust) people that they perceive to be most like them. They also understand people better who come from a similar background and experience.

A cross-cultural team may work in one common language, which may be a second language to some team members. This can create misunderstandings and confusion. If the team members regularly drop into colloquialisms, slang or speaking quickly, some team members may be excluded when they can't keep up. Be careful of team banter and jokes as they rarely translate easily. Ensure that your team pays attention to the needs of the second language team members and are careful with their use of international language. Observe your team's interactions and notice when team members are showing signs of not understanding or keeping up with conversations. Appropriate Routines are also important here. For example, having a Routine of keeping simple minutes of discussions and decisions made in meetings means that team members can review them after the meeting. Share the agenda and materials before the meeting so that team members can read them and prepare. This not only helps non-native speakers, but it will also help the introverts in the team.

When you have a cross-cultural team, you'll need to invest in Relationships in particular. Help people to understand each other at a deeper level and to appreciate the differences within the team. Help them to explore the value of and celebrate the different cultures within the team. There are many tools that help people understand each other better. The aim is not to make everyone the same but rather to use differences as a strength and to increase the perspective the team has.

'During times of discomfort, people revert to their cultural norm. People don't walk around with their cultural background on a badge, therefore you need to approach all conversations with an open mind.'
Paul Howland
NATO Communications and Information Agency
Chief, C2

As leader of a cross-cultural team, you should be aware of cultural differences and help your team to learn about what to look for. Coach team members on how to pay attention to the needs of non-native speakers and how to notice cues for non-understanding or frustration. Help them to adapt their pace and language to be more international. Encourage them to ask questions to understand each other's cultures.

Diversity and inclusion in teams

High-performing teams require diversity and have high levels of inclusion. When we talk about diversity in teams, we mean all types of diversity in humans, such as gender, ethnicity, nationality, sexuality, neurodiversity, physical ability, personality and any other difference that shows up in the human race. When people are different to each other, they think differently about the world. This is what's referred to as 'diversity of thought'. This is an often-untapped superpower in a team, which enables them to solve problems in ways that a homogenous team may not be able to. It's the foundation of innovation and creativity in a team. According to Forbes, 'Nearly 95% of directors agree that diversity brings unique perspectives to the boardroom, while 84% believe it enhances board performance.'[27] We would agree with this and would extend this to all teams, not just boards.

For leaders, it can be harder to manage very diverse teams because Relationships become more complex and you

---

[27] www.forbes.com/sites/forbescoachescouncil/2019/09/13/the-benefits-of-cultural-diversity-in-the-workplace/?sh=4a566a76 71c0

need to understand each team member more fully. It requires deliberate leadership and team effort and skill to flex and adapt to each individual's needs in your team. However, the rewards make it worth it. People really enjoy being part of and building Relationships with a highly diverse group of people. It brings a richness to a team that's not found in homogenous groups. To harness the benefits of a diverse team and take them to high performance, you need to focus on inclusivity.

Inclusive teams recognize that not everyone is the same, that difference is good and people in the team have different needs and approaches to work. For example, a team member who is a parent of small children may have different needs to a team member nearing retirement – they may need flexibility around the school runs, so having team meetings at this time may be excluding to them. A non-native speaker may have different needs to a native speaker – having a team meeting that's all about the spoken word and no written materials may exhaust them. An extrovert may have different needs to an introvert – a meeting that involves lots of listening and no talking may frustrate them. A less confident team member may have different needs to a confident one – they may struggle to speak up in meetings or to share ideas. A female team member may feel that their ideas aren't taken as seriously by the team as her male colleagues'. A team member who has physical difficulties may feel that they can't take part fully in a team-building event involving an obstacle course.

Routines are essential when it comes to creating an inclusive team. Design your Routines carefully so that they enable all team members to be included at critical moments. Regularly check in with your team members, as their needs will change from time to time, to see what's working in terms of your Routines and what's not. Team members won't always tell you when something isn't working for them – they may wait to be asked, so ask them regularly. Ensure that you check in on how inclusive your Routines are specifically. This teaches the team to flex the muscle of continuous improvement, while at the same time emphasizing how important inclusion is in the team. Use the diagnostic tool (see Chapter 1) to help the team to monitor their Edge Dynamics. It's an inclusive tool because it's anonymous to complete and gives everyone a voice about how the team is doing against each of the Edge Dynamics, and a mechanism for voicing insights and actions.

> ### Team composition for high performance – a summary
>
> There are two types of team – simple and complex. Neither type is right or wrong, better or worse. Consider what type of team you have (or want to have) and develop the team accordingly.
>
> Simple teams: all the team members have the same leader but very little, if any, interdependence with each other to get their jobs done.
>
> Complex teams: there are multiple interdependencies among team members, who rely on others in the team to get things done.
>
> Matrix teams: while a useful organizational design, can create complexity for teams in terms of:
>
> - Competing priorities
> - The pull towards the strategic or the tactical
> - A lack of belonging

Project teams: also usually complex because there's interdependency built into the design of the team. They're also invariably a matrix structure. Project teams are also frequently much more dynamic than normal teams as people come and go for various stages of the project.

Size matters in teams and the size of a simple team can be much larger than that of a complex team due to the level of Relationships required.

There are three team distribution types: co-located, virtual and hybrid teams, all of which have different developmental needs and considerations.

Most teams we work with have a mix of cultures within them, whether they're co-located, virtual or hybrid. It's rare to have a mono-cultural team and there are huge benefits to multi-cultural teams. It brings your team a wider variety of perspectives and experiences, which leads to better decision-making and innovation. Having said that, it also can bring challenges, particularly in Relationships, as people tend to like (and therefore trust) people that they perceive to be most like them.

High-performing teams require diversity and have high levels of inclusion. Diversity brings different perspectives too, which can create better outcomes and creates the conditions for high performance.

Conclusion

'Why wouldn't you leverage such a unique competitive advantage that comes from a high-performing team?'

Neil Molyneux
Technical Innovation Group Director, PepsiCo

'High performance' is a term that's thrown around (often quite casually) and doesn't necessarily reflect the true potential of a team. People may not consider what high performance would really mean for a team and how that would be different from good team performance. It's worth spending some time considering what your team could really achieve and what impact it would have on the organization, the individuals in your team and you as their leader if they were performing at their edge.

A high-performing team creates, in the words of Neil Molyneux, 'a unique competitive advantage'. Throughout this book we've provided a framework, tools, strategies and case studies that describe what that competitive edge is and how to get your team there. Everyone wants to perform at their best and everyone deserves a leader who can help them get there. We would say that a high-performing team is the whole team's responsibility, not just the leader's – and you have a fundamental role in creating the conditions for that to happen. When you take this step, and invest in your team's development, you'll unlock the untapped potential you already know is there in your team.

We've established in this book that any leader and their team can achieve good performance, almost by accident.

They can even occasionally glimpse a peak in performance. However, that peak will be fleeting and unsustainable if the Edge Dynamics in the team aren't consistently optimized and aligned. This means that sustainable high performance is achieved through design. It also means setting goals against, measuring, planning and implementing action and reviewing the Edge Dynamics within the team in the same way as you would other organizational initiatives. Team development takes time and effort to effect the change that you, your team and the organization would like to see.

Having read this book, you'll now be aware that your mindset and role as the leader of the team are both extremely important. Your team won't achieve sustained high performance without you. You're the key to unlocking your team's potential and to do this you need to shift your thinking from just managing individuals to leading the polarity of a high-performing team at the same time as managing the individuals within that team. It's a polarity because they require different leadership styles from you – when you're managing an individual you're leading the person in front of you and their individual performance and this is your role alone. When you're leading a team you're now considering the team Edge Dynamics as well, the leadership of which should be shared with your team. Getting the team to take on this shared accountability and to shift their expectations of you as leader in relation to the team takes time. It also can require effort from you in your management of individuals to support the team development process. Within all of this, you may experience moments of vulnerability, particularly if team performance dips. Being aware of your strengths, development areas and impact on the team will enable you to lean into this vulnerability and to use it to develop your team further. It will also help you to challenge the team to take on more of the accountability for the performance of the team itself – this is the key to sustainability. It's inevitable that even the highest-performing teams will experience setbacks, challenges, contextual problems and other issues that test them. A team is only high-performing if they can come out the other side better and stronger than before. This is where Resilience is critical.

So where do you start with your team? As we've said in this book, we would always suggest that you diagnose where your team is now against each of the Edge Dynamics of Reason, Results, Relationships, Routines and Resilience. Once you're clear on where your team is currently, work on the Edge Dynamics that the team thinks is most crucial to them right now. This might not be your lowest-scoring Edge Dynamic and you might want to focus on some quick wins first. To help you decide what to do first, remember you have lots of resources available to you throughout this book, all of which you can download from our website.[28]

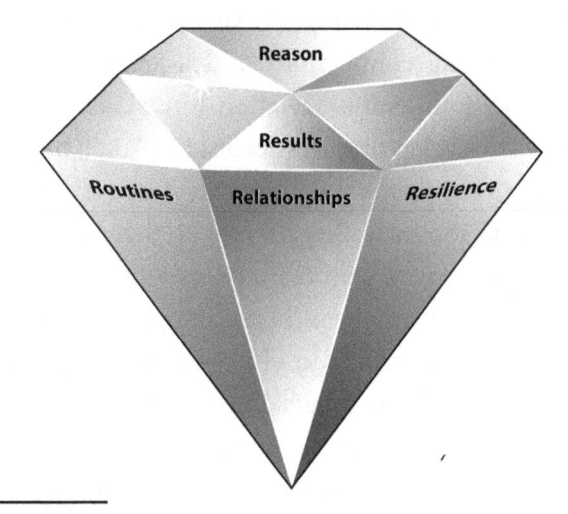

---

[28] www.management-dynamics.com/leading-edge

Reason is your team's North Star and it's often overlooked by teams as its purpose can be misunderstood. Help your team to understand that the team Reason is their *why* and is essential for tapping into their motivation to achieve. Without a compelling team Reason, your team won't achieve their aspirations, as it's impossible to tap into their full potential without a clear and inspirational *why*.

It's essential that a team's Results are crystal clear at the individual and team level. This can also easily be overlooked as teams might think that individual objectives are enough. We know that, to achieve high performance, teams need a greater clarity of their shared team objectives and the associated measures of success. These need to be brief, memorable and inspirational to work. In our experience, you need no more than five 'Big Whats'. Once you have this you can create the opportunities for collaboration where they add the greatest value.

Relationships are complex in teams because people are complex, so it's important to walk before you can run with your team Relationships. Give time and opportunities to make enduring connections and a sense of belonging. Establish the foundation Relationship skills first, before attempting to develop the advanced skills. You'll be in danger of damaging your team's Relationships if you try to force the advanced skills too early. Be patient with this. Little and often is the key to success in your team's Relationships.

Routines are often where there's an opportunity for quick wins. It doesn't take much to change a meeting cadence or agenda, or to establish a decision-making process. In our experience, Routines become 'fixed' and not fit for purpose just because that's the way things have always been done.

Encourage your team to continuously ask, 'Why are we doing this this way?' and 'How could we improve this Routine?' Be prepared to try something out to see whether it might work. Have your own radar for boredom on all the time – notice the signals that your team members (and you!) may be getting bored with a particular Routine. That's your signal to change it in some way. Craft your Routines with the other Edge Dynamics in mind. Consider how Routines can always be used to build Relationships in the team and should connect to Results and the other Edge Dynamics.

Resilience is a fantastic barometer of high performance. It's unusual to have high Resilience and low Reason, Results, Relationships and Routines. Resilience is the key to sustaining high performance, so without it your team's performance will likely be a 'one-off wonder'. Resilience is all about creating a culture of learning. It's about consistently challenging the team to change perspectives and think differently about themselves and their context. Encourage them to be agile and to continuously improve while supporting each other.

This book is about you as a leader of your team. Your role is a special and unique one. You have the ability to achieve amazing Results through your team. You also have the power to get in their way. Of all the leader behaviours we've mentioned in this book, the foundation, so the first place to start, is your self-awareness. Start by looking at the impact you're having on your team and think about your personal journey as a leader. What are your strengths and priorities for development in relation to your team? Recognize that your team is on a journey and so are you as a leader. It's okay to not get it right every time. What's important is that you have a go. Your team will appreciate your efforts immensely!

It's also important to think about the things that impact your team, both positively and negatively, what we call the accelerators and the interferences. Help your team to identify what these are, to establish actions to maximize the accelerators and minimize the interferences. Accept that you as a leader may be an interference yourself and you may feel vulnerable about this. Lean into it and work to minimize this, while maximizing the accelerating leadership behaviours. The team doesn't operate in isolation, so it's essential to look at the conditions and context and monitor where adjustments need to be made.

It's important to pay attention to the team composition – things like team size, distribution, cross-cultural dynamics and diversity of the team all contribute to its success. Use the Edge Dynamics of Reason, Results, Relationships, Routines and Resilience to maximize the team's chances of achieving and sustaining high performance, regardless of their context. They're key levers to maximizing and fulfilling your team's potential.

What one small step will you take now to lead your team to sustainable high performance? Run a team diagnostic to determine how your team is doing against the Edge Dynamics. Use some of the coaching questions with your team. Use some of the Advantycs® tools. Go back to the beginning of the book and complete the Advantycs® Diamond Charter. Take the first step now towards your team's high-performance edge.

Acknowledgements

Many, many people have been involved in some way in the writing of this book, so we'll attempt to thank everyone here.

First of all, to our own high-performing team at Management Dynamics, without whose unwavering support, challenge and ideas, this book wouldn't have been possible. A particular thanks to Peter Firth, who supports us daily on Advantycs®, creating new tools and helping teams with their diagnostics. You rock!

To all of our amazing consultants at Management Dynamics who use Advantycs® every day in their work, supporting teams and leaders. Your constructive and often challenging feedback has been and will always be invaluable to us. A particular mention to Nermeen Amr and Alison Roper, who encouraged us and were there with us right at the beginning of its creation. Thanks to Sarah Hildyard, an amazing team coach – your feedback on the first draft of the book was invaluable. To Lottie Skuthe-Cook, thank you for your feedback and your enthusiasm for high-performing teams. You all continuously stretch our thinking.

To all the leaders of teams that we've supported over the years, thank you – you've embraced our flipcharted ideas and tools with gusto and we've learned so much from you all.

To Frederic Debrosses, thank you for your mentorship, unwavering support and on-target feedback on the book. Your extensive experience and insights challenged our thinking and helped us express our ideas more succinctly.

Thanks to Neil Molyneux – your deep thinking and desire to create high performance is infectious!

To Erik Schmidt, thank you for trusting us with all of your leadership teams worldwide and for your input on the book as we wrote it.

To Paul Howland, your team leadership expertise was invaluable to us in writing this book and your feedback on the book's structure and content was spot on, thank you.

To David Allen, thank you for your wisdom and insight on leading high-performing teams – you took an already great team and used the Advantycs® tools to sustain high performance during significant transformation.

To Adrian Digby, thank you for your fabulous feedback and challenging questions, which developed our thinking and insights.

To Cathrin Westerwelle, your feedback on the case studies in the book was very insightful and helped us shape them – thank you.

To Sue Preston, thank you so much for your insight and leadership lens, which helped us shape the book.

To David Sutcliffe, Alison's amazing husband, whose experience of leading teams and perfectionist tendencies were put to good use several times through the various drafts of the book – thank you many times over.

And finally, to Alison Jones and the team at Practical Inspiration Publishing, a huge thank you for guidance, encouragement, patience and giving us confidence. Thank you to Ivan Butler – you picked up all the mistakes and if any are left they're solely our fault and for that we apologize.

Bibliography

T. Amabile and S. Kramer, 'The power of small wins' in *Harvard Business Review*, May (2011).

C. Aubé, V. Rousseau and S. Tremblay, 'Team size and the quality of the group experience: the more the merrier?' in *Group Dynamics: Theory, Research, and Practice*, 15 (4), 357–375 (2011).

J. Bariso, *Google spent years studying effective teams, this single quality contributed most to their success*. Available from www.inc.com/justin-bariso/google-spent-years-studying-effective-teams-this-single-quality-contributed-most-to-their-success.html

M. Belbin, *Management teams: why they succeed or fail* (2010).

L. Bender et al., 'Social sensitivity correlations with the effectiveness of team process performance: an empirical study', International Computing Education Research Workshop (2012).

K. Blanchard, *Leading at a higher level: how to be a high-performing leader* (2010).

M. Buckingham and A. Goodall, *Nine lies about work* (2019).

M. Campion, G. Medsker and C. Higgs, 'Relations between work group characteristics and effectiveness: implications for designing effective work groups' in *Personnel Psychology*, 46 (4), 823–847 (1993).

R. Cross, R. Rebele and A. Grant, 'Collaborative overload' in *Harvard Business Review*, Jan–Feb (2016).

D. Dias, *The ten types of human: a new understanding of who we are, and who we can be* (2018).

A. Drexler and D. Sibbet, 'Team performance model'.

C. Duhigg, *The power of habit: why we do what we do, and how to change* (2013).

C. Duhigg, *Smarter, faster, better: the secrets of being productive in life and business* (2017).

A. Edmondson, *How organizations learn, innovate, and compete in the knowledge economy* (2010).

G. Elliott, M. Colangelo and R. Gelles, 'Mattering and suicide ideation, establishing and elaborating a relationship' in *Social Psychology Quarterly*, 68, (3) (2005).

G. Elliott, S. Kao and A-M. Grant, 'Mattering: empirical validation of a social-psychological concept' in *Self and Identity*, 3 (4), 339–354 (2004). DOI: 10.1080/13576500444000119

K. Emich and T. Wright, 'The 'I's in team: the importance of individual members to team success' in *Organizational Edge Dynamics*, 45 (1), 2–10 (2016).

Ernst and Young, *The power of many: how companies use teams to drive superior corporate performance* (2013).

S. Gardner and D. Albee, 'Study focuses on strategies for achieving goals, resolutions' (2015). Press Releases. 266.

C. Gersick, 'Marking time: predictable transitions in task groups' in *Academy of Management Journal*, 32 (2), 274–309 (1989).

J. Grenny, *The best teams hold themselves accountable*. Available from https://hbr.org/2014/05/the-best-teams-hold-themselves-accountable

H. Guttman, *Great business teams: cracking the code for standout performance* (2008).

J. Hackman, *Leading teams: setting the stage for great performances* (2002).

K. Hall and A. Hall, *Kill bad meetings: cut half your meetings and transform your productivity* (2017).

M. Hanlan, *High performance teams: how to make them work* (2004).

B. de Jong, K. Dirks and N. Gillespie, 'Trust and team performance: a meta-analysis of main effects, contingencies and qualifiers' in *Academy of Management Annual Proceedings* (2015).

J. Katzenbach, *Peak performance: aligning the hearts and minds of your employees* (2000).

R. Kegan and L. Lahey, *Immunity to change: how to overcome it and unlock the potential in yourself and your organization* (2009).

R. Kegan and L. Lahey, *An everyone culture: becoming a deliberately developmental organization* (2016).

K. Knapp and J. Zeratsky, 'Sprint: how to solve big problems and test new ideas in just five days' (2016).

E. Larson, *New research: diversity + inclusion = better decision making at work*. Available from www.forbes.com/sites/eriklarson/2017/09/21/new-research-diversity-inclusion-better-decision-making-at-work/#285cd6e74cbf

P. Lencioni, *The five dysfunctions of a team: a leadership fable* (2002).

J. Levine and R. Moreland, 'Group socialisation theory and research' in *European Review of Social Psychology*, 5, (1), 305–336 (1994).

G. Lynn and F. Kalay, 'The effect of vision and role clarity on team performance' in *Journal of Business, Economics and Finance*, 4 (3), 473–499 (2015).

S. Marlow et al., 'Does team communication represent a one-size for all approach? A meta-analysis of team communication and performance' in *Organizational Behavior and Human Decision Processes*, 144, 145–170 (2018).

J. Mathieu et al. 'Team effectiveness 1997–2007: a review of recent advancements and a glimpse into the future' in *Journal of Management*, 34 (3), 410–476 (2008).

D. McAdams and E. de St Aubin, 'A theory of generativity and its assessment through self-report, behavioral acts, and narrative themes in autobiography' in *Journal of Personality and Social Psychology*, 62 (6), 1003–1015 (1992).

R. Moreland and J. Levine, 'Socialisation in small groups: temporal changes in individual-group relations' in *Advances in Experimental Social Psychology*, 15, 137–192 (1982).

R. Moreland, J. Levine and M. Wingert, *Creating the ideal group: composition effects at work* (1996).

C. Naquin and R. Tynan, 'The team halo effect: why teams are not blamed for their failures' in *Journal of Applied Psychology*, 88 (2), 332–340 (2003).

A. Pentland, 'The new science of building great teams' in *Harvard Business Review*, April (2012).

J. Polzer et al., 'Capitalising on diversity: interpersonal congruence in small work groups' in *Administrative Science Quarterly*, 47 (2), 296–324 (2002).

M. Rosenberg and C. McCullough, 'Mattering: inferred significance and mental health among adolescents' in *Research in Community and Mental Health*, 2, 163–182 (1981).

R. Ryan and E. Deci, 'Self-determination theory and the facilitation of intrinsic motivation, social development, and well-being' in *American Psychology*, 55 (1), 68–78 (2000).

S. Sinek, *Start with why: how great leaders inspire everyone to take action* (2011).

D. Smith and J. Katzenbach, *The wisdom of teams: creating the high-performance organization* (1993).

E. Sundstrom, K. De Meuse and D. Futrell, 'Work teams: applications and effectiveness' in *American Psychologist*, 45 (2), 120–133 (1990).

R. Susskind and D. Susskind, *The future of the professions: how technology will transform the work of human experts* (2017).

W. Swann et al., 'Finding value in diversity: verification of personal and social self-views in diverse groups' in *Academy of Management Review*, 29 (1), 9–27 (2004).

B. Tabrizi, *75% of cross-functional teams are dysfunctional*. Available from https://hbr.org/2015/06/75-of-cross-functional-teams-are-dysfunctional

B. Tuckman, 'Stages of team development model' (1965).

UK Department of Trade and Industry, 'High performance workplaces – informing and consulting employees (2003).

L. Wiseman, *Multipliers: how the best leaders make everyone smarter* (2017).

D. Witt, *60% of work teams fail – top 10 reasons why*. Available from https://leaderchat.org/2011/11/03/60-of-work-teams-fail—top-10-reasons-why/

A. Woolley et al., 'Evidence for a collective intelligence factor in the performance in human groups' in *Science*, 330 (6004), 686–688 (2010).

Index

1-2-1s 66, 101
80/20 rule 43–44, 166

absence 62
accelerators 164–169, 208
accountability
　'Big Whats' 50–56
　decision-making 67–68
　encouraging direct
　　communication 78–79
　lack of accountability as
　　interference 175
　leadership 150–151, 157-158
　mutual accountability 76
　principles of high-performing
　　teams 6, 7, 10, 11
　reliability-based trust 94–95
　Results 43–44
　Routines 76–79
Advantycs® 18–20, 62, 208
agile mindset 129–130, 159
analogies 131
anti-corruption processes 73
asking for help 102–103
authority gaps 74–75
average, (not) settling for 8

baseline diagnostics 17
behaviours, expected 91–93
behaviours, leaders' 147–161
belonging 108, 180, 186–187, 193
big picture 22, 58–59
'Big Whats' 50–56, 206

BMI (brief, memorable and
　inspirational) 34, 37, 53, 152
breaks, importance of proper 123,
　125
burnout 62, 102, 124, 187
buying in to high performance 10

capability gaps 74
case studies 22–25, 50–51, 90–91,
　99, 106, 150–151, 173, 185,
　189, 193–194
CC box, not using 70
celebrating small wins 123, 159
celebrating successes 6, 17, 159
chair, sharing role of 77–78
clarity 6–7, 44–45, 91, 153–154,
　167–168
cliques/sub-teams 190–191
coaching questions 19–20
collaboration
　'Big Whats' 55–56
　large teams 190, 191
　leadership 154
　over-collaboration 49–50, 55, 56,
　　182, 190
　Relationships 109
　Results 47–49, 206
　simple teams 180–181
collaboration tools 71–72
co-located teams 192–193
commitment 95–99
communication 69–72, 78–79,
　168–169

complex problem-solving xv–xvi,
	xvii, 67, 154
complex teams 181–184, 190
compliance 73
confidence gaps 74–75
conflict within teams 92, 93–94,
	170
consistency 72–73
constructive challenge 76, 88, 93,
	103–106, 151, 156
constructive feedback 101
courage 11–12
COVID-19 64
critical points of failure 127–128,
	135
cross-cultural teams 196–198
culture of learning 129–132

decision-making
	commitment to 95–99
	decision rounds 108
	gaining agreement 95–96
	large teams 191
	leadership 156, 174–175
	Relationships 84
	Routines 66–68
	superior decision-making as
		benefit xvi
decision-tracking 68
'destructive conflict' 92
developing a team 7–9, 12
developmental culture 101
devil's advocate role 105–106
diagnosing your team 16–20
diagnostic tool 18–20
Diamond Charter xxii, 13, 15,
	51–52, 208
difference 89–90, 100–101, 199

direct communication,
	encouraging 78–79
'do more with what you have'
	122–123
duplication of effort 47

Edge Dynamics
	overview 12–25
	complex teams 182
	conditions for success xix–xx
	leaders review all of 159–160
	Relationships as foundation
		84–85, 206
	Resilience scores lowest
		135–136, 207
	simple teams 180
	see also Diamond Charter
email 69–71
emotional energy 137, 139–140
energy, team 124–126, 137–138
Escalation Analysis 176
escalations 73–75, 77, 78
expected behaviours 91–93, 132
experience levels 63–64
experimentation 130
external engagement 75–76, 86,
	172
extra mile, going the 110
extroverts/introverts 63, 65, 109,
	199

'failure' as (non-) concept 124
feedback processes 62, 101, 115,
	132, 151, 169
	see also constructive challenge
flow 126, 167
focus 167
Forbes 198

Index

forced fun 110–111
Formula 1 team thinking 163–177
foundation Relationship skills 87–99
foundation-level leadership skills 160–161
fun 84

Generation Z 29
group think 21, 171–172

high performance, definition of xii–xiii
'holding up the mirror' 132
home working 48, 165
  see also virtual teams
hybrid teams 195–196
hybrid working 48

imperfect contexts 7–8
inclusion 35, 48, 65, 107–110, 157, 198–200
individual benefits of high-performing teams xvii–xviii
induction 89, 109–110, 114, 133, 134–135
innovation xv, 164–165
instant messaging 71
interferences 169–173, 174–176, 208
introverts/extroverts 63, 65, 109, 199

knowledge gaps 74–75
KPIs
  'Big Whats' 52
  not the same as Reason 27–28
  Results 43, 45

laughing together 123
leadership 147–162
  behaviours 147–161
  complex teams 183
  decision-making 67–68
  interferences 174–176
  limiting beliefs 79
  matrix teams 187
  mindset 4–9
  observation skills 137
  operational work 79
  project teams 188
  role-modelling Resilience 140–141
  self-awareness 149–152, 207
  simple teams 180
  workloads 157
leadership teams 183, 190
learning culture 129–132
leavers 114–115, 133–135
loyalty 108

matrix teams 184–187
McKinsey 28, 190
meetings
  online tools 65
  over-collaboration 49
  proactive inclusion 107
  Routines 62, 64–66
  team rhythm 63
mental energy 137, 138–139
mentor roles 128
micromanaging 78, 174
mindsets
  agile mindset 129–130, 159
  leaders 4–9
  team members 9–12
mirror, holding up a 132
mission/vision 34

mistakes, admitting 102
motivation *see* Reason
multi-cultural teams 196–198
multi-lingual teams 197–198
mutual respect and understanding 88

neuroscience of motivation 29–30
new team members 39, 85–86, 89, 101, 109–110, 114, 133–135

observation skills 137
operational/strategic balance 79
opinion-seeker role 109
organization
  organizational benefits of high-performing teams xvi–xvii
  organizational strategy 45–46
  over-collaboration cultures 49
  Reason 34
  Resilience 120–121
  Results 45–46
over-collaboration 49–50, 55, 56, 182, 190
overload 44–45, 56, 65
overwhelm 44–45
ownership of results 5

pace 61–62, 124
permission, giving your team 5–6
personal lives 86–87, 100–101
personal values 31–33, 37, 89, 100–101
personality 63, 88–89
perspective changing 131
  see also constructive challenge; devil's advocate role
physical energy 137, 138
planning workloads 75

poor performance 175
principles of high-performing teams 3–12
prioritization 44–45, 46, 157, 184
processes 72–73
  see also Routines
Productivity Trends Report (2021) 65
project teams 187–188

questioning skills 104, 108–109

radar 11
Reason 27–42, 206
  complex teams 182, 183
  lack of connection to 21
  leadership 152–153
  matrix teams 187
  and Relationships 112–113
  and Resilience 142
  and Results 57
  and Routines 80
  simple teams 180
Relationships 83–118
  cliques/sub-teams 191
  complex teams 182, 183, 190
  cross-cultural teams 196–198
  diverse teams 199
  as foundation 84–85, 206
  leadership 155–156
  matrix teams 184, 186
  poor relationships 21
  and Reason 40
  and Resilience 142
  and Results 57–58
  and Routines 76, 80
  simple teams 180
  virtual teams 194

Index

reliability-based trust 94–95, 100, 136
remote working 47
  see also virtual teams
Resilience 119–144
  as barometer of high performance 207
  complex teams 182, 183
  leadership 158–161
  low resilience 22, 135–136
  matrix teams 187
  and Reason 41
  and Relationships 115–116
  and Results 58–59
  and Routines 80
  simple teams 180
  virtual teams 194
Results 43–60, 206
  complex teams 182
  focus 167
  leadership 153–155
  matrix teams 187
  and Reason 40
  and Relationships 113–114
  and Resilience 125, 142
  and Routines 80
  simple teams 180
rhythm 63–64, 66
role-modelling 140–141, 157
Routines 61–82
  co-located teams 193
  complex teams 182, 183
  cross-cultural teams 197
  diverse teams 199–200
  hybrid teams 195
  large teams 192
  leadership 155-156
  matrix teams 186, 187
  quick wins 206–207
  and Reason 40
  and Relationships 114
  and Resilience 131, 142–143
  and Results 45, 57–58
  simple teams 180
  time zones 196
  virtual teams 194

self-awareness 9, 149–152, 207
shedding 'weight' 166
silos 47, 183
simple teams 179–181, 189
single points of failure 127–128, 135
smarter, working xii–xiii, 10, 30, 122, 123
social activities 110–111
society and Reason 34–35
stakeholders/external engagement 75–76, 86, 172
strategic work 79, 96, 185–186
stress 137, 140, 142
  see also burnout
stretch Relationship skills 100–110
stuck, being 93
substitution 125–126

tactical vs strategic work 185–186
team coaching questions 108–109
team composition 179–201, 208
team dynamics 85, 86
team members
  individual resilience 120, 135–136
  interferences 170–171
  mindsets 9–12
  objectives 44, 46
  Reason 31–33, 37

team objectives 5, 10, 43–44, 45–46, 206
team Reason 33–34, 37–38
team Resilience 121–122, 158
team rhythm 63–64, 66
team size 188–192
team-building days xx, 7, 90, 131
teamworking 78
technology 65, 165–166, 194, 195
time, shortage of 49
time zones 195
timing 9
training 77
trust 94–95, 100–101, 136, 151, 157

upskilling 77

vacations 128

values 37–42
virtual teams 194–195
virtual working 64–65
vision/mission 34
VUCA (Volatility, Uncertainty, Complexity and Ambiguity) xii–xiii
vulnerability-based trust 100–101, 136

WhatsApp 71
why see Reason
winning and learning (all there is) 124
word clouds 39
work planning 75
workloads 10, 75, 77, 97, 102–103, 124, 156